WITHDRAWN

ANNUAL CYCLE OF THE ANNA HUMMINGBIRD

FOOD SUPPLY AND THE ANNUAL CYCLE OF THE ANNA HUMMINGBIRD

BY

F. GARY STILES

UNIVERSITY OF CALIFORNIA PRESS
BERKELEY . LOS ANGELES . LONDON

UNIVERSITY OF CALIFORNIA PUBLICATIONS IN ZOOLOGY
ADVISORY EDITORS: G. A. Bartholomew, J. H. Connell, John Davis,
C. R. Goldman, Cadet Hand, K. S. Norris, Oliver Pearson,
R. H. Rosenblatt, Grover Stephens

Volume 97

Approved for publication July, 14, 1971
Issued May 30, 1973

UNIVERSITY OF CALIFORNIA PRESS
BERKELEY AND LOS ANGELES
CALIFORNIA

◊

UNIVERSITY OF CALIFORNIA PRESS, LTD.
LONDON, ENGLAND

ISBN: 0-520-09419-0

LIBRARY OF CONGRESS CATALOG CARD NUMBER: 76-173901

© 1973 BY THE REGENTS OF THE UNIVERSITY OF CALIFORNIA
PRINTED IN THE UNITED STATES OF AMERICA

CONTENTS

Abstract	1
Introduction	3
Acknowledgments	4
General Biology of the Anna Hummingbird	5
Distribution and habitats	5
Breeding biology	5
Territorial behavior of male Anna Hummingbirds	6
Ecological Backgrounds	9
The chaparral environment	9
The Santa Monica Mountains: topography, climate, and flora	11
Hummingbird food plants of the Santa Monica Mountains	13
Human influences on chaparral ecology	14
Chaparral hummingbirds	16
Methods and Materials	19
Study areas	19
Methods and data presentation	24
Results	27
Comparative chronologies of four annual cycles	27
1966-67 observations	29
1967-68 observations	31
1968-69 observations	38
1969-70 observations	45
Feeding territoriality in the prebreeding season	48
Breeding territoriality of male Anna Hummingbirds	49
Nesting behavior of female Anna Hummingbirds	56
Behavior of prebreeding spring transients	59
Behavior of breeding Costa and Black-chinned Hummingbirds	61
Behavior of juvenile Anna Hummingbirds	65
Behavior of postbreeding summer residents	68
Analysis	71
Food supply and the annual cycle in time and space	71
The initiation of breeding: proximate factors	71
Proximate factors influencing termination of breeding	75
Food supply and seasonal movements	79

Geographic variation in the annual cycle of the Anna Hummingbird . . 81
Influence of man on the annual cycle of the Anna Hummingbird . . 82
The evolution of winter breeding in the Anna Hummingbird . . . 84
    Growth and reproductive seasons of other chaparral organisms . . 84
    Timing of breeding in the Anna Hummingbird: ultimate factors . . 87
    Coevolution of reproductive seasons in *Calypte anna* and *Ribes speciosum* 88
Food supply and the evolution of breeding territoriality 89

Discussion 91
    Food supply, breeding, and seasonal movements of nectar-feeding birds . 91
    Aggressiveness, territoriality, and mating systems of nectarivorous birds . 95
    Nectar-feeding birds and man 99

Summary and Conclusions 101

Literature Cited 105

Plates 111

FOOD SUPPLY AND THE ANNUAL CYCLE OF THE ANNA HUMMINGBIRD

BY

F. GARY STILES

ABSTRACT

The ecology of the Anna Hummingbird (*Calypte anna*) was studied for over three years in the Santa Monica Mountains, California. The overall objective was to assess the role of food supply in determining the spatial and temporal occurrence of territorial behavior, breeding, and seasonal movements. Observations were made in natural chaparral and oak woodland, and in man-altered habitats. Major conclusions of this study include the following:

Male *anna* show two kinds of territorial behavior, here called breeding and feeding territoriality; the behavioral characteristics of each are described in detail. The first heavy winter rains are followed by rapid testicular maturation and the appearance of some breeding behavior in *anna* males, but breeding territories in the chaparral are occupied only as *Ribes malvaceum* comes into bloom there. Full breeding behavior is attained at about the same time each year, despite the variability in timing of rainfall or acquisition of a territory; a response to daylength is suggested. During cold winter months, *C. anna* is the only breeding bird and *Ribes speciosum* practically the only blooming plant in the chaparral. Winter reproduction in either species would be impossible without the other, and a coevolutionary relationship is suggested.

Juvenile *anna* show precocious territorial behavior, and one advantage of winter breeding in *C. anna* is that it may enable some juveniles to become established at good nectar sources before many spring migrant hummingbirds arrive. Defense of breeding territories by *anna* males against increasing numbers of *anna* juveniles and other hummingbirds may become energetically prohibitive as the nectar-rich *Ribes speciosum* stops blooming. Nesting success early in the breeding season determines when juvenile *anna* become numerous in the chaparral, and their disruptive effects on male breeding territoriality inhibit further reproduction, thereby establishing a reproductive feedback system.

Female *anna* often nest near a good nectar source. Their defense of this nectar source early in the nesting cycle resembles male feeding territoriality. Nesting commences following the appearance of male breeding territoriality and the blooming of suitable flowers in nesting areas. Nesting continues until males in breeding condition are no longer available. Young from very late broods may not reproduce the following breeding season.

After breeding, most Anna Hummingbirds move to midsummer feeding grounds in the high mountains; birds remaining in the lowlands generally keep to shaded gardens. In fall some *anna* disperse eastward over the deserts; others return to the lowlands, where they feed mostly at *Nicotiana* and *Eucalyptus*. All return to the chaparral to breed. The timing, direction, and extent of seasonal movements are determined largely by the spatiotemporal distribution of flowers. During the nonbreeding season, male *anna* hold feeding territories at rich nectar sources, but females are nonterritorial.

Man has affected, in varying degrees, the ecology and distribution of every California hummingbird species. The introduction of fall-blooming flowers has doubtless increased the total *anna* population. Man has affected the occurrence of breeding and seasonal movements in space but not in time; nesting success of *anna* in natural and man-altered habitats is similar.

INTRODUCTION

THE ANNA HUMMINGBIRD, *Calypte anna*, is the only hummingbird common year-round north of the Mexican boundary. Most of its range lies within the state of California, long a major center of ornithological activity. Because of its accessibility, the Anna's general biology is the best known of any hummingbird. The major features of its annual cycle, including breeding and seasonal movements, were well known to Grinnell (1908) and Willett (1912). Numerous early writers have given accounts of its courtship, nesting, feeding, plumage, and general behavior (summarized by Woods, 1940). More recently, territorial behavior and interspecific competition have been studied in the Anna and other hummingbirds by Pitelka (1951*a*, *b*) and Legg and Pitelka (1956) in the breeding season, and by Ortiz (1967) in the nonbreeding season. Williamson (1956) attempted to relate molt and gonadal activity to behavioral events in the annual cycle of *C. anna*. The work of these authors provides a solid foundation for the present study of the ecological factors that regulate the timing of the annual cycle in the Anna Hummingbird.

My major objective is to examine, on a seasonal basis, the effects of weather and food supply upon territoriality, reproduction, and population movements. In effect, I shall attempt to interpret the ecology of *C. anna* in terms of food requirements and availability, and the way in which these influence the spatial and temporal occurrence of other activities. This is a particularly pertinent approach to the study of hummingbirds, whose food requirements are relatively higher than for other birds because of their small size and high metabolic rate. Ecologically speaking, hummingbirds tend to be more closely tied to their food sources than are other birds: relatively more of their activities, in space and time, may be oriented with reference to a food source.

Territorial behavior is a case in point: defense of food sources is probably more frequent and widespread in hummingbirds than in any other bird group. The mating territory of males of most North American hummers is set up with reference to a food supply (Pitelka, 1942), and one of my major objectives is to clarify the relations between defense of food and breeding territoriality

Wolf's (1969) definition of territory, in somewhat modified form, is appropriate here: a territory is a fixed, localized area in which the resident restricts access to an environmental or social resource by other individuals, thereby helping to satisfy its own biological requirements. This definition regards territoriality as a resource-directed phenomenon, and focuses attention on what Brown (1964) has termed the "economic defendability" of the resource. In energetic terms, this is the ratio between energy gained through exclusive (or preferential) use of the resource to the energetic cost of defending it. The present report will focus on factors such as weather, distribution and abundance of food, and competition, which may effect this energy balance.

ACKNOWLEDGMENTS

This study was completed as partial fulfillment of the requirements for Doctor of Philosophy at the University of California at Los Angeles. I wish to first thank Thomas R. Howell, chairman of my doctoral committee, for advice and encouragement throughout this study. My thinking on hummingbird ecology has benefited from stimulating discussions with R. C. Lasiewski, G. H. Orians, F. I. Ortiz-Crespo, O. P. Pearson, F. A. Pitelka, E. O. Willis, and L. L. Wolf. During the lengthy course of this work, I have greatly appreciated the companionship and constructive criticisms of my fellow graduate students, especially G. S. Benson, T. W. Brown, B. Heinrich, L. F. Kiff, F. H. Pough, and C. H. Trost. For advice on handling of data, I thank M. L. Cody and D. L. Landenberger. I am indebted to the Los Angeles Department of Water and Power for permission to work at Franklin Canyon and Stone Canyon Reservoirs. The caretakers of these reservoirs, R. C. Wells and C. H. Armstrong, have been extremely cooperative and helpful. For assistance in plant identifications, I am grateful to M. E. Mathias and members of the Stone Canyon gardening staff. M. J. Borowski graciously supplied records of the UCLA Weather Station. For access to museum specimens under their care, I wish to thank E. N. Harrison, N. K. Johnson, W. E. Lanyon, J. G. Miller, and J. R. Northern. Other observers who kindly supplied information on the Anna Hummingbird include R. Adams, S. Wells, Mr. and Mrs. R. Witzemann, and R. Wright. I thank M. L. Cody and R. I. Yeaton for permission to cite their unpublished data on chaparral insects. The aerial photographs were made with the aid of R. Shallenberger.

During 1967-68 and 1968-69, my work was supported by a National Science Foundation Predoctoral Fellowship. During the final stages of preparing the manuscript for publication, I was supported by a Chapman-Naumberg Postdoctoral Fellowship from the American Museum of Natural History.

I am pleased to thank the members of my doctoral committee, Professors G. A. Bartholomew, N. E. Collias, T. R. Howell, R. C. Lasiewski, H. J. Thompson, and B. M. Wenzel, for their critical reading of the manuscript and their help in numerous other ways. I am very grateful to Julia L. Kiff and Aileene H. Stiles for typing the manuscript.

Finally, I wish to give special thanks to my friends and colleagues Larry L. Wolf and Lloyd F. Kiff for consistently stimulating discussion, advice, criticism, and encouragement.

GENERAL BIOLOGY OF THE ANNA HUMMINGBIRD

Distribution and Habitats

The Anna Hummingbird breeds along the Pacific coastal slope of North America from northwestern Baja California north to San Francisco Bay, and in the foothills of the Coast Ranges and Sierra Nevada surrounding the Great Central Valley of California. Elevations of breeding localities run from sea level up to 600 meters in the north, and up to 1,800 meters on warmer slopes of the southern Coast Ranges (Grinnell and Miller, 1944). The breeding range of *C. anna* is virtually coincident with the warmer and drier parts of the California chaparral. Typical breeding habitat consists of hilly or mountainous terrain, in which hillsides and canyon slopes are covered by chaparral, with oak or sycamore woodland growing in the canyon bottoms (see below). The Anna Hummingbird is also common in dooryards, parks, and gardens, both inside and outside of the breeding season.

Following the breeding season there is a midsummer movement to the higher mountains, up into coniferous forests and mountain meadows at elevations of up to 1,800 meters in the north and 2,700 meters in the south (Grinnell and Miller, 1944). This vertical migration was first noticed by Grinnell (1908), and was further documented by Willett (1912) and Grinnell and Swarth (1913). The hummingbirds return to the lowlands in September and October, apparently when cold cuts down the food supply at high elevations. At this time there is a dispersal of the population north and west along the coast and out to the Channel Islands, and southeastward into the deserts at least as far as southern New Mexico and northwestern Sonora (Grinnell and Miller, 1944; van Rossem, 1945). However, by January virtually the entire population returns to California to breed.

Breeding Biology

In *Calypte anna*, as in all hummingbirds, the female builds the nest, incubates, and rears the young with no direct assistance from the male. There is little or no contact between the sexes beyond the actual mating itself. During most of the breeding season, the sexes occupy different habitats: males hold breeding territories on chaparral-covered slopes, while females nest in the canyon-bottom woodlands. The following account of courtship and nesting is drawn from my own observations, and from the accounts of Dawson (1923), Legg and Pitelka

(1956), and Woods (1940). A more detailed description of courtship and other displays of *C. anna* will be published elsewhere (Stiles and Ortiz MS).

Courtship and mating are brief and violent, involving first a chase of the female by the male. When the female stops and perches the male may give one or more dive displays, in which he climbs to a height of 60 to 110 feet and then executes a near-vertical dive, swinging up sharply at the bottom with a loud squeak produced by vibrations of the rectrices. Following the dive(s), the female may drop down into thick shrubbery or to the ground, to be quickly followed by the male; here, precopulatory displays by the male and finally copulation may take place. Following copulation, male and female go their separate ways. A male may fertilize several females and a female may mate with several males in the course of the breeding season.

At the time of mating the female has her nest already at least partly built, but she may add materials until well into incubation. Depending partly on the time of year, a female may spend from 3 days to 2 weeks or more building a nest (Legg and Pitelka, 1956), but the average is about 1 week. The clutch is invariably two (as in all hummingbirds), and incubation requires 14 to 19 days. The nestling period ranges from 18 to 23 days. The young remain dependent upon the female for the first few days after fledging, but achieve independence within 1 to 2 weeks. During the course of a breeding season, a female typically raises two broods; should a nesting fail, she usually tries again within about 10 days.

TERRITORIAL BEHAVIOR OF MALE ANNA HUMMINGBIRDS

The male Anna Hummingbird shows two types of territorial behavior in the course of the annual cycle, which may be called breeding and feeding territoriality. These will now be described in some detail since the kind of territorial behavior a male shows is often a good indicator of whether or not he is in breeding condition. Since this study seeks to identify the ecological factors that influence the initiation and termination of breeding, some behavioral indicator of reproductive status is extremely important.

Breeding territoriality is characteristic of the reproductive season, and a male holding such a territory is almost certainly in breeding condition (cf. Williamson, 1956). Pitelka (1951) divides the territory into two concentric zones: the core area and the buffer zone. The core area averages about $\frac{1}{4}$ acre in size and contains most or all of the perches upon which the bird spends most of his time, often advertising his presence by singing, and from which he fares forth to feed, display, or chase intruders. The vegetation of the core area is usually relatively low and uniform in height, so that the male can scan most or all of the area from each perch. Often the core area consists of a patch of lower shrubs with taller bushes roundabout, in effect a natural "arena." One may define the buffer zone as that region surrounding the core area, within which the resident male will consistently attack an intruding hummingbird. The outer edge of the buffer zone is ill-defined, and fluctuates according to weather and foliage conditions, and even time of day. The size of the buffer zone thus varies greatly, but is usually between 5 and 15 acres.

The core areas of *anna* breeding territories are truly "exclusive" areas, within which the resident will attack and chase any other hummingbird. The buffer zones of adjacent males sometimes overlap, and levels of defense in the buffer zone fall off rapidly and often irregularly toward the periphery. Probably the most constant features of the core areas of *anna* territories are the physiognomy of the vegetation and the availability of suitable perches, but wherever possible males appear to choose perches such that they can control a food supply on territory, as will be discussed in detail below.

Behaviorally, an *anna* male on a breeding territory is characterized by persistent singing from exposed perches through most of the day, and by the frequency and great length of chases employed in territorial defense. Dive displays are also diagnostic of a male in breeding condition; their function is mostly one of intimidation, notwithstanding their importance in courtship. Dive displays are given to any hummingbird perched in or near a male's territory, and also to other kinds of birds perched in the core area. Advertising flights, in which a male flies, singing, in wide circles high over his territory, are also characteristic of breeding territoriality.

During the nonbreeding season, male Anna Hummingbirds generally hold feeding territories. A feeding territory consists of one to several flowering plants, plus a perch or two in or near them. Territory size is determined mostly by the distribution of food and the level of competition for it. A male will attempt to defend at least enough of a nectar source to support him for an entire day. The richer and/or more localized the food source, the smaller will be the average minimum territory size. The maximum amount of food that a male can defend reflects the amount of competition: if a large enough number of birds compete for a sufficiently small or localized food source, this maximum may fall below the minimum amount of food needed by a male to maintain himself. Under these circumstances, territoriality will no longer be economically feasible, in the sense of Brown (1964).

Perhaps the most important ecological distinction between breeding and feeding territoriality is that the former involves defense of an area per se, within which food may or may not be present; the latter involves only defense of the food source itself. A breeding male will attack any hummingbird flying over his territory, even at heights of 100 feet or more. The airspace (or area between food plants, if any) of a feeding territory is usually not defended. Anna males on feeding territories sing much less than when on breeding territories, and generally use inconspicuous perches, often within the food plant itself. They are much more likely to chatter at other hummingbirds flying by, and less likely to chase them unless they start to feed at one of the defended plants. Chases are short: seldom will an intruder be pursued beyond the bounds of the territory itself. Display flights almost never occur, and then they are usually incomplete.

A level of defense comparable to that of feeding territoriality is shown during the reproductive season by Anna males at regularly visited food sources outside of their breeding territories: the "Type 1 territoriality" of Aldrich (cf. Pitelka, 1942). In most cases, these males are not present at the food sources regularly or consistently enough to be considered resident there, and the term "territory" is something of a misnomer; the important factor is that they are the dominant birds when present.

ECOLOGICAL BACKGROUNDS

The Chaparral Environment

The Anna Hummingbird is almost entirely restricted in its breeding distribution to the California chaparral, and its annual cycle is very closely tied to that of the chaparral itself. Therefore, it is crucial to consider in detail the distinctive seasonal rhythms of climatic conditions, and plant growth and flowering in the chaparral.

The California chaparral grows under what is often called a "Mediterranean" climate: mild, rainy winters and hot, dry, nearly cloudless summers. The temperature rarely falls much below freezing even in the coldest months (January through March), but frequently exceeds 32°C in the hot months of July, August, and September. Annual rainfall averages about 250 to 750 millimeters, mostly falling between December and March (see fig. 1). Soil moisture, high during the rainy season, drops to low levels within two months of the last heavy rains (Hanes, 1965). Regardless of the amount of rain during the winter, nearly all soil moisture has dissipated by the end of the following summer (Pillsbury et al., 1953). Plant growth is largely dependent on soil moisture, and is generally halted from midsummer until the start of the winter rains, even if fall temperatures are favorable. When the rains come, growth in most plants may be further retarded until spring by low temperatures (Miller, 1947).

Most areas where chaparral grows are hilly or mountainous, with steep slopes and shallow, rocky soils. Slope and exposure have very pronounced effects on both climate and vegetation. South-facing slopes have higher maximum temperatures than do north-facing slopes, but about the same minimum temperatures, and therefore a greater temperature range. Evaporation may be 15 percent greater on southern exposures than on northern ones (Miller, 1947), and northern and eastern exposures may receive 20 percent more rain than do southern and western ones (Bauer, 1936). The composition and structure of the vegetation may be radically different on north- and south-facing slopes (Cooper, 1922; Bauer, 1936; Miller, 1947). Temperature inversions frequently occur in the deep, steep-sided canyons; canyon bottoms may have minimum temperatures several degrees cooler than the surrounding slopes (Cole, 1967).

Fire is also an integral part of chaparral ecology, and toward the end of the long summer drought lightning-set fires are frequent. Postfire succession also shows pronounced slope effects, with vegetation on northern exposures showing quicker regeneration and greater structural and taxonomic diversity than that on south-facing slopes (Hanes and Jones, 1967).

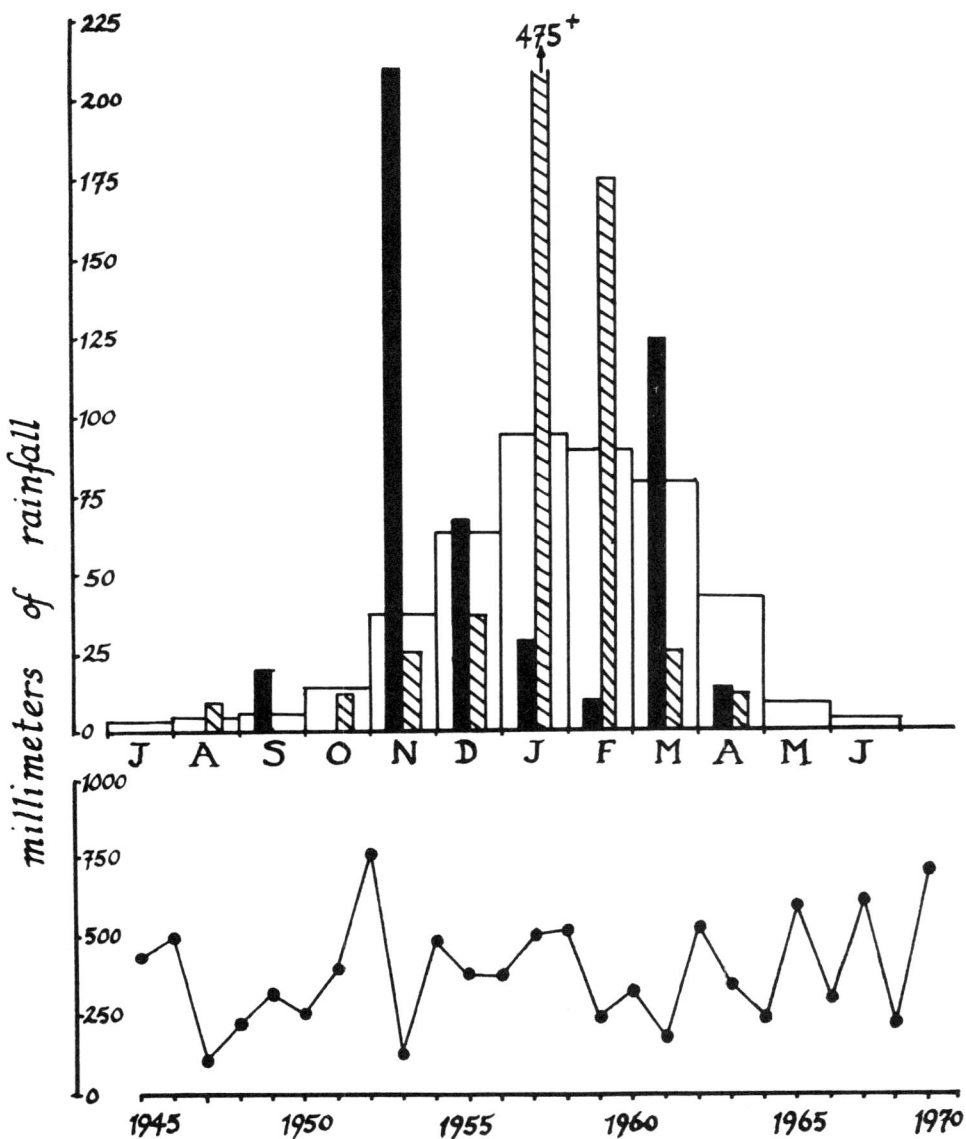

Fig. 1. Rainfall patterns recorded by the UCLA weather station.
Upper graph: open bars—25-year average monthly rainfall; solid bars—monthly rainfall in 1967-68; hatched bars—monthly rainfall in 1968-69.
Lower graph: variation in annual rainfall at UCLA over a 25-year period.

The dominant life form of chaparral vegetation is perennial, sclerophyllous or "hard-leaved" shrubs. This name refers to the thick, hard cuticle of the leaves of many chaparral shrubs, an adaptation for conserving moisture during the long summer drought (Cooper, 1922). Chaparral shrubs must also be able to grow and photosynthesize under a wide range of temperatures, and in poor and rocky soils. Growth and flowering of most chaparral plants takes place in the spring, especially March through June (cf. fig. 3). During the summer and fall, as moisture becomes limiting, flowering declines and most nonsclerophyllous plants lose their leaves. In some plant species, notably those of the genera *Ribes* and *Arctostaphylos*, the first winter rains trigger growth and flowering, which continue through the coldest months of the year. The blooming of these plants is an important factor in the ecology of *Calypte anna*.

A striking feature of the chaparral climate is its irregularity. The first heavy rains, upon which so much depends, may fall anytime between October and February (Miller, 1947; Hanes, 1965; see also figs. 1 and 12). The last strong rains, of great importance in maintaining soil moisture, may cease as early as February or as late as May (Bauer, 1936). Total annual rainfall also varies greatly; in the records of the UCLA weather station over the last 25 years, annual rainfall has varied irregularly between 119.5 and 795.0 millimeters with an average of 444.2 mm (fig. 1). Prolonged spells of hot, dry weather, in which temperatures may reach $25°$ to $30°C$, may occur during any month of the winter. Thus, any plant or animal which initiates breeding directly or indirectly in response to the winter rains must have special adaptations for responding to temperature, moisture, and photoperiod.

THE SANTA MONICA MOUNTAINS: TOPOGRAPHY, CLIMATE, AND FLORA

The Santa Monica Mountains are a part of the outer coast ranges of California. The east-west axis of the range runs some 80 kilometers along the line of $34°5'N$ latitude, between $118°20'$ and $119°5'W$ longitude. To the southeast and east lies the Los Angeles Basin, to the north the Simi Hills and the San Fernando Valley, and to the west the Oxnard Plain. Just beyond the San Fernando Valley and within a mile of the Santa Monica Mountains at their eastern end, are the much taller San Gabriel Mountains, with peaks of up to 3,000 meters. It is here that many of the *anna* of the Santa Monica Mountains area probably spend the hot summera months. To the south of the Santa Monica Mountains lies the Pacific Ocean, and none of the major peaks are more than 8 kilometers from the sea. The topography is rugged, and the southern slopes of the mountains rise up steeply from the coast to heights of 600 to 1,000 meters (fig. 2). The chief geological formations of the range are of Triassic, Cretaceous, and Miocene age, but the mountains themselves were formed by an anticlinal uparching in the late Pleistocene (Bauer, 1936).

Almost no part of the Santa Monica Mountains is more than 15 kilometers from the sea, and this has important effects on the climate and flora. Coastal breezes are usual, and fog is frequent along the seaward side of the mountains,

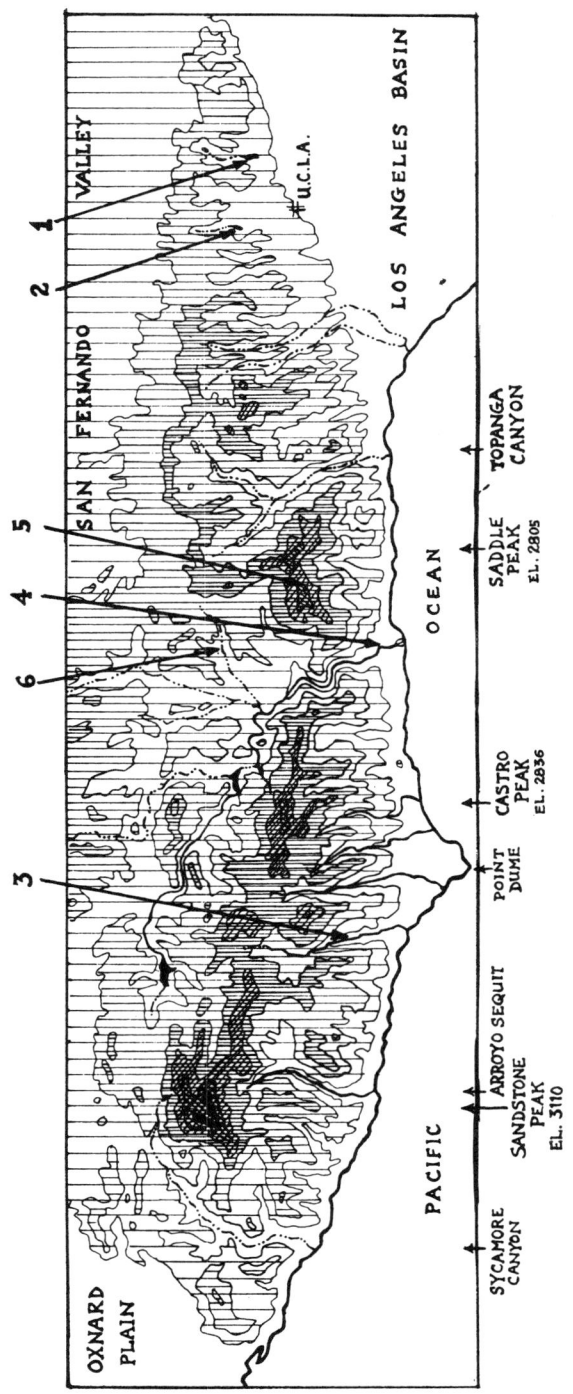

especially in the winter months. Due to orographic effects, precipitation is much greater in the higher parts of the mountains than along the immediate coast (Bauer, 1936). By the time the coastal winds have passed over the mountains they have lost most of their moisture, creating a rain shadow over the northern slopes and interior valleys. These areas are the driest in the mountains, and have the greatest temperature extremes. Next driest, but much cooler, is the coastal district (Cole, 1967). For further discussion of the climate of the Santa Monica Mountains and vicinity, see Hanes (1965), Cole (1967), and Bauer (1936).

There are five major natural plant communities in the Santa Monica Mountains region. Along the coastal front of the mountains below 2,000 feet, and over much of the northern slopes, lies the coastal sage or "soft" chaparral, dominated by woody subshrubs such as *Salvia* and *Diplacus*, and shrubs like *Rhus laurina* and *Artemisia californica*. The true "hard" chaparral, with woody shrubs like *Adenostoma*, *Ceanothus*, and *Arctostaphylos* predominating, occurs mostly in the higher parts of the mountains. There is a broad, fluctuating ecotone between coastal sage and chaparral; often the former extends well above 2,000 feet on south- and west-facing slopes, while the latter extends much lower on northern and eastern exposures. In some areas, coastal sage species will occur early in postfire succession, to be replaced later by chaparral species (Bauer, 1936; Miller, 1947). Oak woodland, dominated by *Quercus agrifolia*, occurs commonly in canyon bottoms and may extend upwards on protected north- or east-facing canyon walls. In this report, the term "chaparral," used without qualification, refers to both coastal sage and "hard" chaparral; only in direct or implied comparisons to coastal sage is its meaning restricted to the "hard" chaparral. A riparian woodland dominated by *Platanus* and *Alnus* may also occur in canyons with more or less permanent streams. In the canyons and valleys to the north of the main ridge is found a dry grassland (perhaps better called oak savanna, as *Quercus lobata* is common), sprinkled here and there with dense patches of *Salvia*.

HUMMINGBIRD FOOD PLANTS OF THE SANTA MONICA MOUNTAINS

Probably the most important food plants of the Anna Hummingbird during the breeding season are the two species of *Ribes* (plate 1), which are most common in canyon bottoms and sheltered locations in chaparral and coastal sage, especially on northern and eastern exposures. *Ribes* is particularly abundant in disturbed chaparral; both species occur in early successional stages on north-facing slopes, where they may later be shaded out by taller shrubs (Hanes and

---

Fig. 2. Contour map of the Santa Monica Mountains, showing locations of major study areas. Contour interval: 500 feet. Scale: 1 inch equals approximately 7 miles.
    Study areas: 1—Franklin Canyon; 2—Stone Canyon; 3—Trancas Canyon; 4—Malibu Creek; 5—Murphy Ranch; 6—Cold Creek Canyon.

Jones, 1967). *R. malvaceum* begins blooming immediately following the first winter rains. *R. speciosum* leafs out at this time, but blooms later; it is in full flower in the cold months of January through March, when it is almost the sole nectar source for *anna*. Dawson (1923) states that it is upon *R. speciosum* "that *C. anna* depends for her early nesting." In the higher and cooler chaparral, mostly above 2,000 feet, a manzanita, *Arctostaphylos glauca*, also blooms during the cold months and is much visited by hummers at this time.

Important spring-blooming food plants are *Diplacus longiflorus* and the various species of *Salvia*. *Diplacus* is common in coastal sage and in the warmer parts of the chaparral, where not shaded out by taller shrubs. The various shrubby *Salvia* are abundant in coastal sage and interior valleys. The herbaceous *S. spathacea* is found in deep canyon bottoms. Of the several species of *Penstemon* present, the shrub *P. cordifolius* is the most frequented by hummingbirds, and is common in canyons and on protected slopes in the eastern part of the mountains. *Penstemon* and *Trichostema lanatum*, of the dry interior chaparral, are the most important native food plants of early summer. During late summer, the only native flower much used by hummingbirds is *Zauschneria*, the two species of which occur in sheltered canyon bottoms and slopes. In most areas, however, *Zauschneria* is not common enough to support more than a few individual birds. Thus, taking into account only native plants, late summer and fall would appear to be periods of food scarcity for chaparral hummingbirds. This is the time when *anna* and other hummers move up into the mountains, then disperse eastward across the deserts. Some aspects of the ecology and flowering of hummingbird food plants in the study area are summarized in table 1.

Human Influences on Chaparral Ecology

Man has had a very great effect upon the landscape of the Santa Monica Mountains and surrounding regions. Man-created and man-altered habitats, and introduced food plants, play an integral part in hummingbird ecology in this area. Indeed, I doubt very strongly if any hummingbird population in California goes through an annual cycle without coming into more or less extensive contact with man or his influence. This influence extends even to natural habitats; fire prevention in the Santa Monica Mountains has very probably altered the composition and structure of the chaparral to some degree.

California was renowned for its gardens even during the Spanish colonial period, and since that time few areas on earth have undergone so extensive and successful a program of plant introductions and naturalizations (Padilla, 1961). Presently a wide variety of flowers is available to hummingbirds in gardens and other plantings, often ornithophilous species from other parts of the world: *Strelitzia* and *Aloe* (South Africa); *Abutilon, Nicotiana, Fuchsia*, and *Cestrum* (South America); *Eucalyptus* and *Callistemon* (Australia); and many others

TABLE 1

ECOLOGICAL AND FLOWERING CHARACTERISTICS OF IMPORTANT HUMMINGBIRD FOOD PLANTS IN THE SANTA MONICA MOUNTAINS

Plant species	Habitat	Distribution	Abundance	Growth form	Nectar secretion	Number of flowers	Blooming season
Native species							
Ribes malvaceum	CSW	X	C	s	I	3	X-III
R. speciosum	CSW	X	C	s	III	3	XII-V
Arctostaphylos spp.	C	X	C	s	I	3	XII-II
Diplacus longiflorus	S(C)	X	C	ss	I	1-2	III-VI
Salvia mellifera	S	X	C	s	I	3	III-VI
S. leucophylla	SO	X	C	s	I	2-3	IV-VII
S. apiana	SO	Y	U	s	I	1-2	V-VII
S. spathacea	W	Y	U	h	II	1	III-V
Scrophularia californica	SW	X	C	h	I	1	IV-VI
Dudleya spp.	S(W)	X-Y	C-U	ss	I	1	V-VI
Silene laciniata	W(S)	Y	U-R	h	I	0	IV-VII
Penstemon cordifolius	S	Y	C	s	III	2	V-VIII
Castilleja spp.	SC	X	U	h, ss	I, II	0-1	IV-VIII
Zauschneria spp.	WS	Y	U	ss	II	1-2	VII-XI
Trichostema lanatum	SO	X	C-U	s	II	1-2	IV-VI
Naturalized species							
Nicotiana glauca	E(S)	X	C	s(t)	II	2-3	II-XI
Eucalyptus globulus	EG(CSW)	X	C	t	IV	2-4	IX-V
Cultivated species							
Abutilon spp. & varieties	G	Y	C	s	IV	2	III-VI*
Fuchsia spp. & varieties	G	X	C	s	III-IV	1-2	II-I
Callistemon speciosum	G	X	C	s(t)	III	2-3	III-X
Pittosporum undulatum	G	X	C	s, t	I	2-4	II-VI
Cestrum elegans	G	Y	U	s	II	3	XI-V*
Heliconia sp.	G	Y	C-U	h	III	1	VII-XII
Strelitzia reginae	G	X	C	h	IV	0-1	X-VII*
Erythrina crista-galli	G	Y	U	t	IV	3-4	VII-XI
E. caffrae & coralloides	G	X	C	t	IV	3-4	I-V
Hibiscus rosa-sinensis	G	X	C	s, t	II	2	II-X
Jacobinia spp.	G	Y	R	s	I	2	XII-V
Hamelia patens	G	Y	U-R	s	II	3	IV-VIII
Heuchera sp.	G	Y	C	h	I	0-1	IV-VI

ABBREVIATIONS

Habitat: C—chaparral; S—coastal sage; E—edges, roadsides, etc.; W—woodland (oak or riparian); O—oak savanna and northern valley; G—Gardens and cultivated areas.

Distribution: X—widely distributed; Y—locally distributed (within favorable habitat).

Abundance: C—common; U—uncommon; R—rare.

Growth form: h—herb; s—shrub: ss—subshrub, t—tree.

Nectar secretion (in microliters/flower/day): I = 1-10; II = 10-25; III = 25-50; IV = 50.+

Number of flowers (on mature specimen at full bloom): 1 = 1-10; 2 = 10-100; 3 = 100-1000; 4 = 1000+.

Blooming seasons given as roman numeral of month; asterisk designates a plant that blooms all year, in which case the numerals refer to the months of peak flowering.

(see table 1). From the 1850s on, the extensive citrus orchards (locally less extensive now than formerly, however) have provided a major springtime nectar source for breeding and migrating hummingbirds (Woods, 1927).

As far as hummingbirds are concerned, the most important introduced plants by far are *Nicotiana glauca* and *Eucalyptus globulus*. Thus is because they have become quite naturalized and now are often found far from areas of present human habitation, and also because they bloom during the fall and winter, at a time when native flowers are at a low ebb. *Nicotiana* was brought in during the eighteenth century by the Spanish, and probably escaped from cultivation in the early nineteenth century (Padilla, 1961). It is now found commonly along roadsides, in disturbed areas, and openings in the chaparral; it is sometimes one of the first plants to invade by seed following fire. Over 30 species of *Eucalyptus* trees have been introduced into California, but *E. globulus* is the only one to become extensively naturalized. Introduced in 1856 (Butterworth, 1964), it had become a prominent part of the landscape by the 1880s, and was very extensively planted during the "Eucalyptus craze" of the early 1900s (Padilla, 1961).

Chaparral Hummingbirds

I have recorded 6 species of hummingbirds in the Santa Monica Mountains. Three species breed: *Calypte anna*, *C. costae*, and *Archilochus alexandri*. *Selasphorus rufus* and *S. sasin* are both spring migrants and summer postbreeding visitors, while *Stellula calliope* has only been seen during spring migration, usually associated with, and much less common than, *Selasphorus rufus*. *Calypte anna* is the only species present in numbers year-round, though it is much less common in summer and early fall than at other times. It is also the largest hummer of the area (table 2). The Anna is the most widely distributed hummingbird in the mountains, particularly during the breeding season, when it is locally common in both chaparral and coastal sage. Those *C. anna* remaining in the area during the summer are found in gardens or *Nicotiana* stands.

Calypte costae, the Costa Hummingbird, and *Archilochus alexandri*, the Black-chinned Hummingbird, arrive in March and April, respectively, and May is the peak of breeding for both species. By mid-July, most *alexandri* have departed for the higher mountains, along with *anna*; most *costae* remain in the chaparral during the summer. Both species leave for their wintering grounds in Mexico during September.

The Allen Hummingbird, *Selasphorus sasin*, is a very uncommon spring transient in the chaparral during January and February; it migrates mostly along the coast. From June onward, it is a common postbreeding visitor. *S. rufus*, the Rufous Hummingbird, passes through the Santa Monica Mountains in large numbers in March and early April, en route to breeding grounds as far north as Alaska. By late July, postbreeding birds are common, especially in stands of

Nicotiana. As most of the postbreeding *Selasphorus* are juveniles, one cannot distinguish species in the field at this time. All *Selasphorus* have left for their Mexican winter quarters by mid- to late October.

TABLE 2

ECOLOGICAL AND MENSURAL CHARACTERISTICS OF HUMMINGBIRDS OF THE SANTA MONICA MOUNTAINS

Species	Status and abundance[1]	Measurements (millimeters)[2]				Weight (grams)[4]			
		culmen length[3]		wing length		N males		N females	
		males	females	males	females				
Calypte anna	PR(C), BR(A)	18.82 ± 0.96	19.79 ± 0.86	49.76 ± 0.95	49.26 ± 1.01	36	4.40 ± 0.34	31	4.08 ± 0.38
Calypte costae	BR(C), PR(R)	17.77 ± 0.72	18.47 ± 0.98	44.06 ± 0.76	44.72 ± 0.88	25	2.98 ± 0.25	19	3.25 ± 0.26
Archilochus alexandri	BR(A), SR(R)	19.26 ± 0.78	22.29 ± 1.02	42.19 ± 1.13	46.06 ± 1.26	18	3.09 ± 0.21	17	3.36 ± 0.22
Selasphorus s. sasin	ST(R), SR(C)	17.15 ± 0.63	18.72 ± 0.73	38.03 ± 0.85	41.40 ± 0.90	11	2.85 ± 0.21	12	3.25 ± 0.21
Selasphorus rufus	ST(A), SR(A)	17.27 ± 0.69	18.90 ± 0.72	40.35 ± 0.86	44.39 ± 0.83	14	3.07 ± 0.16	14	3.41 ± 0.25
Stellula calliope	ST(U)	14.91 ± 0.82	16.72 ± 0.61	38.55 ± 0.70	41.57 ± 0.91	22	2.53 ± 0.30	16	2.94 ± 0.28

1. PR—permanent resident; BR—breeding resident; ST—spring transient; SR—postbreeding summer resident. A—abundant; C—common; U—uncommon; R—rare.
2. Mean and standard deviation. N = 25 in all cases; adults in fresh plumage.
3. Length of total culmen, not exposed culmen (cf. Baldwin et al., 1930).
4. Mean and standard deviation. Adults in breeding condition—no migratory fat deposits.

METHODS AND MATERIALS

The present study was carried out between January 1967 and June 1970 inclusive, with interruptions during April-May 1967, August-September 1968, July-August and late December 1969, and March-April 1970. Thus, for every month except August, I have observations from at least two different years. The most intensive observations were made during the 1967-68 and 1968-69 breeding seasons.

Study Areas

Several localities in the Santa Monica Mountains were singled out for intensive study, although I also made periodic tours through much of the mountains to keep a general check on hummingbird activity. Each of these study areas (see fig. 2) was chosen to emphasize a different aspect of the ecology of *anna* and other chaparral hummingbirds. The two sites at which I made extensive observations through the entire year were Franklin Canyon and Stone Canyon, both in the eastern end of the mountains. At both sites, there is a wide variety of habitats and food sources available to hummingbirds. They are also close enough to UCLA that the university weather station data can be appropriately used (fig. 1). In an area of such rugged topography as the Santa Monica Mountains, there are great local variations in amount and pattern of rainfall.

Most of my observations on breeding territoriality in male hummingbirds were made at Franklin Canyon. The chief study site was a steep-sided ridge extending southward down from the main backbone of the mountains (plate 2 and fig. 10). The canyon bottom is about 150 meters above sea level; the highest point on the ridge is some 250 meters, but adjacent ridges are higher, rising to over 300 meters. Along a fire road running 1 kilometer along the ridgetop both species of *Ribes* were abundant, resulting in a high density of territorial *C. anna* males. Vegetation of the ridge contains both chaparral and coastal sage elements. The former are dominant on the eastern slope, where frequent tall *Ceanothus* and *Heteromeles* bushes are mixed with smaller shrubs, giving a very broken and irregular shrub canopy. Oak woodland extends part-way up the canyon wall in sheltered locations. *Ribes* is much more abundant on this side of the ridge. On the west-facing slope, coastal sage elements like *Salvia mellifera*, *Eriogonum fasciculatum*, and *Rhus laurina* predominate. Blooming seasons of some of the dominant plants in the Franklin Canyon chaparral and coastal sage are presented in figure 3.

Franklin Canyon Reservoir occupies most of the canyon bottom area. The surrounding slopes are covered by chaparral and oak woodland, but there are

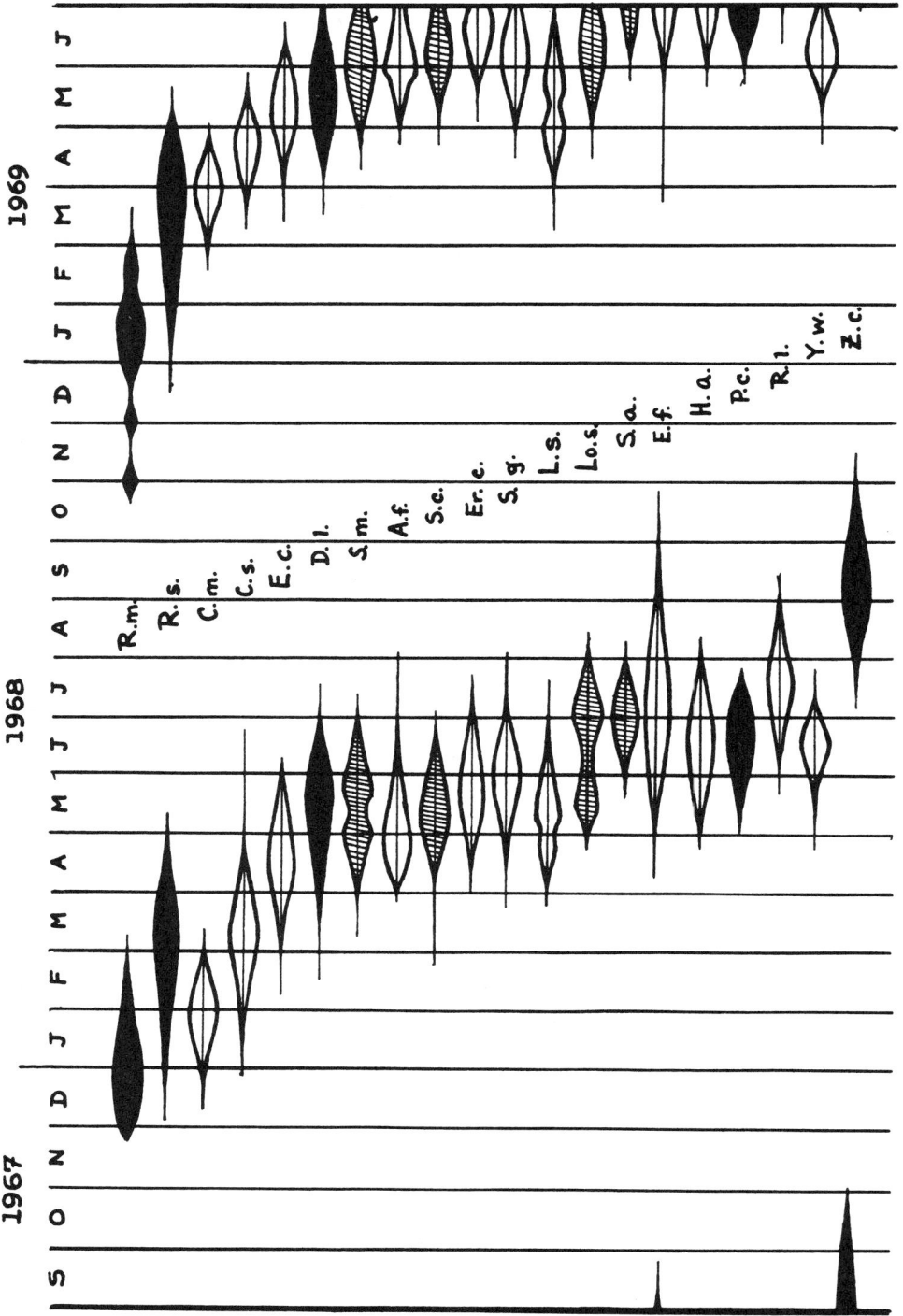

gardens and groves of the introduced Deodar (*Cedrus deodara*) at both ends of the reservoir. Along roadsides or at the edge of the chaparral are more or less extensive stands of *Nicotiana glauca*. Below the dam at the lower end of the reservoir is a 5-hectare citrus orchard. The Franklin Canyon area thus offers a fairly good cross-section of the kinds of habitats available to hummingbirds on the coastal slope of Southern California, and movements between different habitats and flowers can be studied on a daily and seasonal basis.

Stone Canyon Reservoir is some 8 kilometers west of Franklin Canyon, and in the same sort of terrain (plate 3A). Of greatest interest here is an extensive oak-alder grove, augmented by redwoods and deodars, at the lower end of the reservoir (plate 3B). In the shade of the trees are planted many flowers which provide good hummingbird foraging: *Abutilon*, *Fuchsia*, *Heliconia*, *Cestrum*, and others. Just outside the main "garden grove" area are plantings of *Hibiscus rosa-sinense*, *Strelitzia reginae*, and a very large grove of *Eucalyptus globulus*. At several points around the edge of the gardens, thick stands of *Nicotiana* grow. The surrounding canyon walls support a broken chaparral in which *Ribes* is well represented. Stone Canyon is notable for the large amount of hummingbird nesting activity in the garden grove, which is structurally similar to native woodland, but with the food supply greatly augmented. I made most of my observations on nesting behavior of *C. anna* females here. Like Franklin Canyon, Stone Canyon is also a good area in which to study seasonal movements of hummingbirds between habitats, and shifts in food preferences. At no time during the year are there fewer than 2 or 3 hummingbird food plants in bloom (fig. 4) and blooming seasons of most cultivated or introduced species are very long relative to those of native flowers (cf. figs. 3 and 4).

Fig. 3. Blooming seasons of representative chaparral plants at Franklin Canyon, September 1967 through June 1969. Graphs are derived from data on flowering percentages (see text).

Solid figures: flowers pollinated largely or exclusively by hummingbirds.

Hatched figures: flowers visited frequently by hummingbirds, but predominantly insect-pollinated.

Open figures: flowers rarely or never visited by hummingbirds, pollinated by insects or other agents.

Abbreviations:

R.m.—*Ribes malvaceum*
R.s.—*Ribes speciosum*
C.m.—*Ceanothus megacarpus*
C.s.—*Ceanothus spinosus*
S.c.—*Scrophularia californica*
Er.c.—*Eriophyllum confertiflorum*
S.g.—*Sambucus glauca*
L.s.—*Lotus scoparia*
Lo.s.—*Lonicera subspicata*
S.a.—*Salvia apiana*

E.c.—*Encelia californica*
D.l.—*Diplacus longiflorus*
S.m.—*Salvia mellifera*
A.f.—*Adenostoma fasciculatum*
E.f.—*Eriogonum fasciculatum*
H.a.—*Heteromeles arbutifolia*
P.c.—*Penstemon cordifolius*
R.l.—*Rhus laurina*
Y.w.—*Yucca whipplei*
Z.c.—*Zauschneria cana*

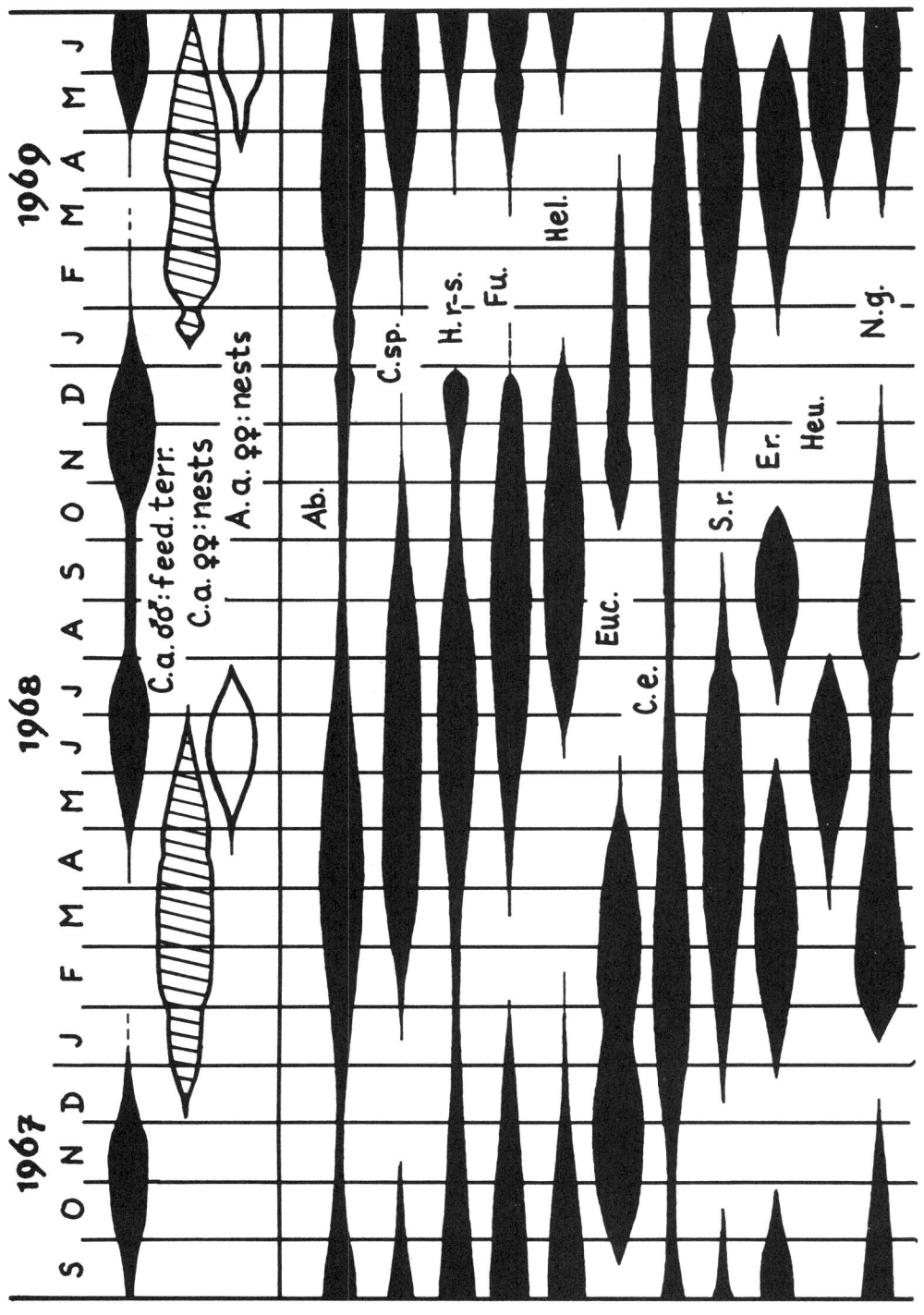

I made fairly extensive observations on nesting in *C. anna* at Trancas Canyon, in an area relatively untouched by man, for comparison with the situation at Stone Canyon. Trancas is a deep, steep-sided canyon with a well-developed oak woodland at the bottom, as well as numerous sycamores (*Platanus racemosa*) along Trancas Creek (plate 4). The canyon bottom is only about 25 to 50 meters above sea level, but the surrounding ridges rise to over 600 meters. The canyon walls are covered by very thick hard chaparral on eastern and northern exposures; coastal sage elements are more prevalent on southern and western slopes, especially near the sea. *Ribes* is rare on the canyon slopes, but fairly common in the canyon bottom oak woodland. *Diplacus* and several species of *Salvia* are abundant in the area.

The Murphy Ranch, just below Saddle Peak, is the highest of my study sites, being almost all above 600 meters in elevation (see fig. 2). The vegetation of the area has been well described by Bauer (1936) and Hanes (1965). It suffices here to state that the dominant vegetation on sloping terrain is a very old and thick hard chaparral; there is also a fairly extensive patch of oak woodland. *Ribes* is relatively uncommon in the area; the major hummingbird food plant during the winter months is a manzanita, *Arctostaphylos glauca*. Observations on territoriality and nesting were made here, for comparison with lower-elevation areas.

Localities visited mostly during the nonbreeding season included Encinal and Cold Creek canyons, and Malibu Creek. Extensive stands of *Nicotiana glauca* bloomed through the summer and fall at each of these sites. The first two areas consisted of roadside *Nicotiana* stands surrounded by essentially undisturbed chaparral. The Malibu Creek locality was in an area of more extensive human disturbance, including plowed fields and housing developments. Also present here was a large grove of *Eucalyptus*.

Unfortunately, practically all of the *Nicotiana* at Malibu Creek was swept away in the floods of January 1969. In the disastrous fires that swept the Santa Monica Mountains in the autumn of 1970, virtually all of the vegetation of the Murphy Ranch, Malibu Creek, and Cold Creek Canyon localities was destroyed.

Fig. 4. Hummingbird activity and blooming of cultivated and naturalized food plants at Stone Canyon, September 1967 through June 1969. Graphs of blooming seasons derived from subjective estimates of flowering (see text). Note the effects of freezing weather in late December 1968, and heavy rains in late January 1969, on blooming of several species.

Abbreviations:
  Ab.—*Abutilon* spp. & varieties
  C.sp.—*Callistemon speciosum*
  H.r-s.—*Hibiscus rosa-sinensis*
  Fu.—*Fuchsia* spp. & hybrids
  Hel.—*Heliconia* sp.
  Euc.—*Eucalyptus* spp., especially *E. globulus*
  C.e.—*Cestrum elegans*
  S.r.—*Strelitzia reginae*
  Er.—*Erythrina* spp.
  Heu.—*Heuchera* sp.
  N.g.—*Nicotiana glauca*

Methods and Data Presentation

At each of the main study areas, I made periodic general surveys of hummingbird activity and blooming of food plants. During the breeding season, I visited Franklin and Stone Canyons for 2 to 6 hours at least once every 10 days, and Trancas Canyon for 4 hours or more once every 2 weeks. Time of day and weather data were recorded during each visit. Most observations were made during early to midmorning or mid- to late afternoon, hummingbird activity being greatest at these times. Table 3 summarizes the dates of important events in the annual cycle of *anna* during the 3 years of my study.

During each visit to an area, I plotted locations of all territorial males and all active nests on mimeographed maps of each site. All regularly used perches and food plants of territorial male *anna* were located. Figure 10 shows the locations of the core areas of *anna* breeding territories along the ridgetop trail at Franklin Canyon, during 3 different years. Wherever possible, I determined the food plants used by each nesting female, and ascertained the stage of each nest. After 2 or 3 visits to a nest, I could usually estimate the dates of initiation of nest-building and fledging by use of the average values for the duration of building (7 days), incubation (16 days), and nestling (20 days) periods (see above). These fledging dates can be used in estimating nesting success; if the young in a nest disappear much before that date, the nesting was probably not successful. It is well known that young hummingbirds outgrow the nest cup just before fledging, trampling down and fouling the nest rim (Bent, 1940). Since young at this stage can also fly for at least short distances (perhaps well enough to escape a predator at the nest), a nest with flattened and befouled rim probably fledged young. Of course, a sure sign of a successful nesting is the presence of fledglings nearby; a nest emptied or destroyed early in the nesting cycle is a certain failure. Figure 6 gives the estimated starting dates and probable fates for the 81 *anna* nests found in Stone and Trancas Canyons during 1967-68 and 1968-69. Nesting success of *anna* and *alexandri* in the present study is compared with that of other North American species in table 10.

For the most important chaparral plants, a quantitative index of blooming was devised. During each visit to an area, I counted the flowers on certain predetermined individuals of each plant species. From these counts I calculated a "flowering percentage" for each plant species at each visit. Data on blooming seasons of a series of representative chaparral plants, compiled from flowering percentages, are presented in figure 3. Figures 5 and 7 show blooming of important food plants in relation to hummingbird activity in the Franklin Canyon chaparral in 1967-68 and 1968-69, respectively. For the cultivated and naturalized food plants at Stone Canyon, flowering data was derived from subjective estimates rather than flower counts; the blooming of these plants in relation to hummingbird activity is presented in figure 4. The graphical representations of hummingbird activity in these figures summarize observations on numbers, territoriality, and nesting, collected during general surveys and censuses (see below).

Daily nectar production was sampled with 25- or 50-microliter capillary tubes for each food plant, using bagged flowers (to prevent removal of nectar by birds or insects). These data are presented in table 1, along with other parameters of each food plant relevant to hummingbird exploitation: patterns of abundance, number of flowers per plant, growth habit, and blooming season. For plant identifications and nomenclature, I used Raven and Thompson (1966), McMinn (1959), or Jepson (1925), in that order.

To obtain quantitative data on hummingbird activity, I set up two census routes at Franklin Canyon. For each census, I walked the route at a steady rate to insure uniform coverage, and noted the location and activities of every hummingbird seen or heard. No attempt was made to distinguish individuals, but species and sex were determined wherever possible. The ridgetop trail constituted one census route: I started at the north end, walked to the south end (just over 1 kilometer) and returned, the entire census consuming about 45 minutes. During the 1968-69 breeding season, trail censuses were taken between 0800 and 1000, at intervals of 3 to 10 days (fig. 9). The other census route was laid out around Franklin Canyon Reservoir and down into the orange grove below the dam. All available habitats were represented: chaparral, oak woodland, gardens, *Nicotiana* scrub, groves of planted conifers, and the orange grove. The census route was about 4 kilometers in length, and required 3 to 4 hours to travel. These reservoir censuses were taken monthly or semimonthly between September 1968 and June 1969, and are summarized in table 6.

During trail and reservoir censuses and general surveys, I recorded all aggressive activity seen, and tried to ascertain the species and sex of all individuals involved. Table 11 brings together data for those aggressive encounters (usually chases, sometimes supplantings) in which both participants were identified. I also attempted to determine how the amount of food controlled by a breeding male *anna* might influence his other activities. The amounts of aggressive activity in a 3-hour period by two male *anna* controlling different amounts of food (*Ribes*) are compared in table 9. In table 8, the number of trips to food sources outside the breeding territory in relation to the amount of food on territory, is presented for 4 *anna* males at Stone Canyon.

Timing of events of the *anna* breeding cycle was studied in relation to rainfall, blooming of food plants, and numbers of competing hummingbirds. Figure 12 summarizes data on initiation of breeding territoriality by *anna* males relative to the early winter rains and blooming of *Ribes* in 3 different years. During the fall and winter of 1968-69, I studied the relation between testicular maturation, molt, and initiation of breeding territoriality in male *anna*. For this study, 21 male *anna* were collected in the Santa Monica Mountains, using mist nets, blowgun, and shotgun. Data on testis volume, molt stage, and territorial status of these birds is presented in figure 8. Figure 13 shows numbers of competing *Selasphorus* migrants and juvenile *anna* and blooming of food plants, in relation to decline of breeding territoriality in *anna* males in late spring.

When I wished to follow the activities of a particular hummingbird, I marked the bird in question with 1 or 2 spots of colored airplane dope on the back. Each individual marked was given a unique color combination. Birds were captured by mist-netting, usually at feeding bushes. During the 1967-68 season, I marked 5 territorial male and several juvenile *anna*, as well as a number of spring migrant and summer resident *Selasphorus*. I was able to follow the activities of these individuals until they began to molt or left the area.

Identification of female and juvenile hummingbirds presented a major problem at first, especially as information in published field guides and other references is mostly inadequate or misleading. I was therefore obliged to develop my own techniques for field identification of these birds, based upon vocal and behavioral as well as morphological characters (Stiles, 1971b). Females and immatures of the two *Selasphorus* species are quite indistinguishable in the field, but I was able to determine species, age, and sex of birds in the hand (Stiles, 1972).

RESULTS

Comparative Chronologies of Four Annual Cycles

The annual cycle of the Anna Hummingbird can be divided into three more or less overlapping 'seasons': prebreeding, breeding, and postbreeding. The prebreeding phase lasts from early or mid-October until the first heavy winter rains, which fall sometime between November and January in most years. The *anna* in the high mountains return to the lowlands, or disperse eastward over the desert. After mid-October, the Anna is the only hummingbird regularly present in the Santa Monica Mountains area, all others having gone south for the winter. The red feathers of gorget and crown of most *anna* males are molted at this time.

The breeding season usually begins in November or December with the movement of male *anna* onto breeding territories, followed within a few weeks by the beginning of nest building by the females. It ends with the males abandoning their breeding territories in April and May, and the females ceasing nesting activities between May and July. The breeding season of the females thus lags behind that of the males, in some years by over a month.

The postbreeding season includes the hottest part of the year, and most *anna* desert the chaparral for the high mountains. Those birds that remain in the low-

TABLE 3

Timing of Major Events in the Annual Cycles of *Calypte anna* and Other Chaparral Hummingbirds During Four Years

Event of annual cycle	Year and date			
	1966-67	1967-68	1968-69	1969-70
First heavy winter rains	—	XI:18-22	X:24	XI:5-6
First blooming of *Ribes malvaceum*	—	XI:24	XI:1-10	XI:7
First breeding territories occupied by *C. anna* males	—	XI:24	XI:28	XI:14
Definitive breeding territories first occupied by *C. anna* males	—	XI:24	XII:31	XI:14
Final or maximum number of breeding territories occupied	by I:20	I:21	I:31	XII:16, II:10
Ribes malvaceum at full bloom	I:7-15	I:14	I:21	XII:6-10
First blooming of *Ribes speciosum*	before I:5	XII:23	I:10	XII:16
Ribes speciosum at full bloom	III:1-10	III:11-15	III:25—IV:1	—
First *C. anna* nesting activity seen	—	XII:8	I:6	XII:3

TABLE 3 (*continued*)

Event of annual cycle	Year and date			
	1966-67	1967-68	1968-69	1969-70
First recorded *C. anna* eggs	ca. XII:25	ca. XII:28	I:20	ca. XII:5
First juvenile *C. anna* seen	II:11	II:7	III:12	I:19
Juvenile *C. anna* common in chaparral	III:10-15	III:13	IV:16	before IV:12
First spring migrant *C. costae* seen	III:26	III:11	III:14	———
First *C. costae* nesting activity seen	———	III:20	III:27	———
First *C. costae* juvenile seen	———	V:19	V:2	V:3
C. costae juveniles common in chaparral	by VI:11	V:30	not by VI:6	VI:4
First spring migrant *A. alexandri* seen	———	IV:7	IV:11	IV:15
First *A. alexandri* nesting activity seen	———	IV:17	IV:14-20	IV:21
First recorded *A. alexandri* eggs	———	IV:25	IV:22	IV:28
First *A. alexandri* juvenile seen	VI:22	VI:25	none by VI:6	VI:16
Extreme dates: spring migrant *S. rufus*	III:11-?	III:9–IV:14	III:3–IV:22	? - IV:13
Peak numbers: spring migrant *S. rufus*	III:15 & 25	III:31–IV:3, IV:10	III:15 & 20, IV:7	———
First postbreeding *Selasphorus* seen	before VI:11	V:22	V:11	VI:17
Postbreeding *Selasphorus* common	ca. VII:20	VI:1	not by VI:6	not by VI:27
Ribes speciosum finishes blooming	———	V:10-20	V:20-25	V:3-10
Most *C. anna* males molting	by VI:11	V:10	V:7-17	V:3
Most *C. anna* males abandon breeding territories	———	IV:10-20	IV:20-25	before IV:12
Latest *C. anna* males holding breeding territory	———	V:7	V:17	V:3
Latest recorded eggs laid: *C. anna*	ca. V:26	V:5	ca. V:22	ca. V:5
Latest nest-building seen: *C. anna*	———	V:25	V:28	V:10
Last *A. alexandri* seen in fall	IX:23	gone before IX:20	———	———
Last *C. costae* seen in fall	IX:14	IX:25	———	———
Latest date postbreeding *Selaphorus* common	X:2	X:10	before X:10	———
Last *Selasporus* seen in fall	X:11	XI:11	X:10	———

Dates are given as month (roman numeral); day (arabic numeral).

lands are found in cooler, shaded spots—gardens, or thick oak woodlands. Large numbers of postbreeding *Selasphorus*, as well as many *costae*, are found through the summer at more open locations, especially in *Nicotiana* stands. After mid-July, most of the *alexandri* as well as some *Selasphorus* have also left for the mountains. Most of the annual molt of body and flight feathers of adult *anna* takes place during the postbreeding phase, which lasts from June or July to September or early October.

The following observations are presented in hummingbird-years, not calendar years; each year contains prebreeding, breeding, and postbreeding "seasons." The timing and duration of these seasons vary from year to year, as will be discussed below. Table 3 summarizes differences in timing of important events of the annual cycle of the Anna Hummingbird in four different years.

1966-1967 OBSERVATIONS

My observations during 1966-67 were rather fragmentary, and during the breeding season consisted largely of exploring and mapping study areas, setting up census routes, locating feeding areas, etc. Observations were made from 5 January through 26 March and 11 June through the end of September of 1967, thus encompassing the middle of the breeding season and most of the postbreeding season.

Breeding season.—In mid-January I began regular observations at Franklin Canyon. A census along the first 800 meters of the ridgetop trail produced 7 male *anna* on breeding territories, a density comparable to that of succeeding years. *Ribes malvaceum*, in full bloom in January, declined rapidly thereafter. *Ribes speciosum* was just starting to flower in January and reached full bloom in early March. At this time, *anna* juveniles were moving into the chaparral in increasing numbers, and the first migrant *Selasphorus rufus* were seen. Numbers of *rufus* reached peaks of 15-20 birds on several occasions in mid- to late March. By late March, local concentrations of *anna* juveniles were also seen. *Ribes speciosum* was approaching the end of its blooming season at this point, but *Diplacus* was blooming vigorously and still on the increase.

Observations on nesting were extremely fragmentary during spring 1967. Seven nests were found in 3 visits to Stone Canyon and one to Trancas. The earliest nest found was one at Stone Canyon that fledged young on 11 February; therefore that clutch had probably been completed around 25 December. Nests in all stages were still present when observations were concluded in late March. A single *anna* nest with newly hatched young was found at Stone Canyon on 13 June, but was empty on 20 June.

Postbreeding season.—By early June, *anna* males were no longer holding breeding territories, and all individuals seen were in heavy molt. Those males still in the chaparral usually perched low and inconspicuously and seldom sang. Several male *anna* had already moved into gardens such as those at Stone Canyon and set up feeding territories at flowers like *Abutilon* and *Fuchsia*. No adult male *anna* were seen in the chaparral after 11 June, even though food was still abundant: *Diplacus*, *Salvia mellifera*, and *Nicotiana* were just past full bloom, and flowering of *Penstemon cordifolius* was rapidly increasing. The commonest chaparral hummingbird at this time was *costae*, males of which still held breeding territories through early July. I saw very few *alexandri*, but this may have reflected my lack of familiarity with its behavior and vocalizations rather than an actual scarcity of birds. *Penstemon* reached full bloom in early July and was much visited by *costae*, especially juveniles, and by a few juvenile *anna*.

Postbreeding *Selasphorus* (mostly juveniles) invaded Franklin and Stone Canyons in mid-July, settling mostly in stands of *Nicotiana*. By late July, most native food plants had declined greatly in flowering except *Zauschneria* which was just beginning to bloom. The major food source outside of gardens was *Nicotiana*, which had another peak of flowering in early August.

During the hot days of July and August, practically the only hummingbirds in the chaparral at midday were *costae* (mostly juveniles) and juvenile *Selasphorus*. Most *anna* and *alexandri* spent the midday hours in shady gardens or woodlands, and ventured out into chaparral or *Nicotiana* areas only in early morning and late afternoon (see table 4). Those *anna* holding feeding territories were found almost exclusively in shady gardens, at cultivated flowers. The few *anna* (usually juveniles) territorial at *Nicotiana* had nearby perches in groves of trees or large, shade-producing bushes. By contrast, many juvenile

TABLE 4

MIDSUMMER DISTRIBUTION OF HUMMINGBIRDS BETWEEN DIFFERENT HABITATS AND FOOD PLANTS

	Hummingbirds						
	C.a. ♂♂	C.a. juv.	A.a. ♂♂	A.a. juv.	C.c. ♂♂	C.c. juv.	Selas. juv.

A. Variation in numbers of hummingbirds at *Nicotiana* stands in chaparral with time of day: combined results of trail censuses of 25 July through 10 August 1967.

Time of census							
Early morning (before 0700)	4	9	1	4	3	11	16
Midday (1100–1400)	0	1	0	1	1	9	14
Evening (after 1800)	7	11	0	5	6	14	19

B. Locations of birds holding feeding territories in surveys of 22–26 August 1967, Franklin and Stone Canyons.

Shaded gardens and cultivated flowers	7	3	1+	1	0	0	1?
Chaparral and roadsides: *Nicotiana*	0	1	0	3	2	10	9

costae and *Selasphorus* maintained feeding territories at *Nicotiana*, and seemed less affected by the midday heat than did *anna* (table 4).

Postbreeding and juvenile *costae* and *alexandri* left the study area by mid- to late September. Juvenile *Selasphorus* (mostly or entirely *rufus*) were fairly common until early October, but disappeared soon thereafter (see table 5).

1967-68 OBSERVATIONS

My 1967-68 observations are continuous with those of 1966-67, and run through 29 July 1968. They encompass the entire prebreeding and breeding seasons, and most of the postbreeding season. Between January and April 1968, much of my efforts were devoted to studies of time and energy budgets and territorial defense of a single male *anna*. This work is presented elsewhere (Stiles, 1971a), but relevant observations on territoriality are included in the present report. Figure 5 shows blooming of chaparral food plants during 1967-68 in relation to hummingbird activities; blooming of cultivated flowers at Stone Canyon is given in figure 4.

Prebreeding season.—With the departure of postbreeding summer residents, *anna* began moving into *Nicotiana* stands in numbers, and many adult and first-year males established feeding territories in good *Nicotiana* patches. The only native chaparral flower blooming at this time was *Zauschneria*, which occurred in small, scattered clumps and was visited by small numbers of nonterritorial birds—females and first-year males.

TABLE 5

NUMBERS OF HUMMINGBIRDS HOLDING FEEDING TERRITORIES AT *Nicotiana* AT MALIBU CREEK DURING CENSUSES OF LATE SUMMER AND EARLY FALL 1967

Date of census	Blooming of *Nicotiana*	Hummingbirds					
		C.a. adult ♂♂	C.a. first year ♂♂	A.a. immature ♂♂	C.c. adult ♂♂	C.c. immature ♂♂	Selas. immature
12 August	good bloom	0	3	3	2	8	5
24 August	near peak of bloom	1	2	1+	1?	ca. 10	15-20
27 September	good bloom	4	2	0	0	0	23
10 October	good bloom	5	4	0	0	0	9+
19 October	fair bloom	8	7	0	0	0	0
30 October	poor bloom	2	4	0	0	0	0
10 November	nearly done blooming	0	2	0	0	0	0

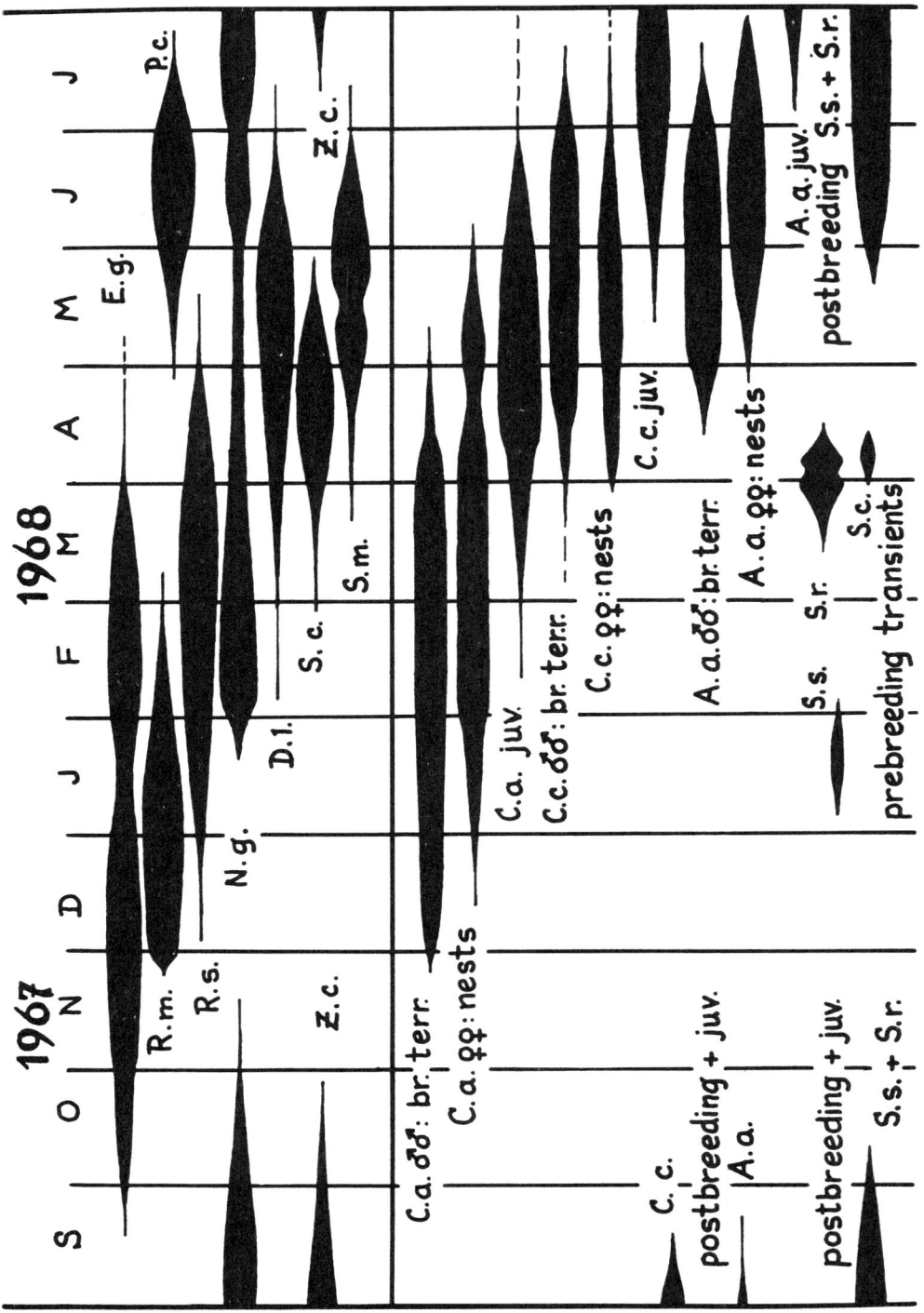

The flowering of *Nicotiana* declined rapidly in October, and it had effectively ceased to bloom be early November. The number of male *anna* holding feeding territories at *Nicotiana* declined concurrently, and many males apparently moved first into gardens and other cultivated areas, setting up new feeding territories at cultivated flowers. By November, no native food plants of any kind were blooming, and the chaparral had been entirely deserted by hummingbirds. At this time, *Eucalyptus globulus* began to flower in numerous localities in the Santa Monica Mountains, and soon became the most important single food plant for hummingbirds in the region.

Breeding season.—The first heavy winter rains fell on 18-22 November, following several months of hot, dry weather. On 24-25 November *Ribes malvaceum* was starting to bloom vigorously in several localities, and *anna* males were setting up breeding territories in these areas. Males were singing from prominent perches in their new holdings; dive displays and advertising flights, nonexistent the week before, were now frequent. Suddenly, the breeding season had begun (cf. fig. 12).

Ribes malvaceum reached full bloom by mid-January, at which time *R. speciosum* was also beginning to flower vigorously. The number of *anna* breeding territories in the chaparral reached a maximum of 12 along the ridgetop trail at Franklin Canyon (fig. 10) and 6 in the Stone Canyon hillside chaparral (see also table 3). In February, the flowering of *speciosum* continued to increase, while that of *malvaceum* declined rapidly. The number of territorial *anna* males in the chaparral changed relatively little but there were local shifts corresponding to changes in the distribution of the food supply.

The first nest-building activity by female *anna* was seen on 8 December at Stone Canyon, and 20 December at Trancas Canyon. The first recorded clutches of eggs at these localities were laid around 28 December and 15 January, respectively. Nesting was somewhat retarded at Stone Canyon until male *anna* abandoned their feeding territories and moved into the chaparral, which some birds did not do until December or even January. The peak of the nesting season was roughly late February through March, when at any given time there were upwards of 4 or 5 and 10 or 11 active nests at Trancas and Stone Canyons, respectively

---

Fig. 5. Hummingbird activity and blooming of chaparral food plants at Franklin Canyon, September 1967 through July 1968. Graphs of blooming seasons derived from data on flowering percentages (see text). Graphs of hummingbird activities summarize data from general surveys, censuses, and other observations presented in text.
Abbreviations:
    E.g.—*Eucalyptus globulus*. Other abbreviations of plant names as in figs. 3 and 4.
    C.a.—*Calypte anna*   S.s.—*Selasphorus sasin*
    C.c.—*Calypte costae*   S.r.—*Selasphorus rufus*
    A.a.—*Archilochus alexandri*   S.c.—*Stellula calliope*
    juv.—juveniles   br. terr.—breeding territories

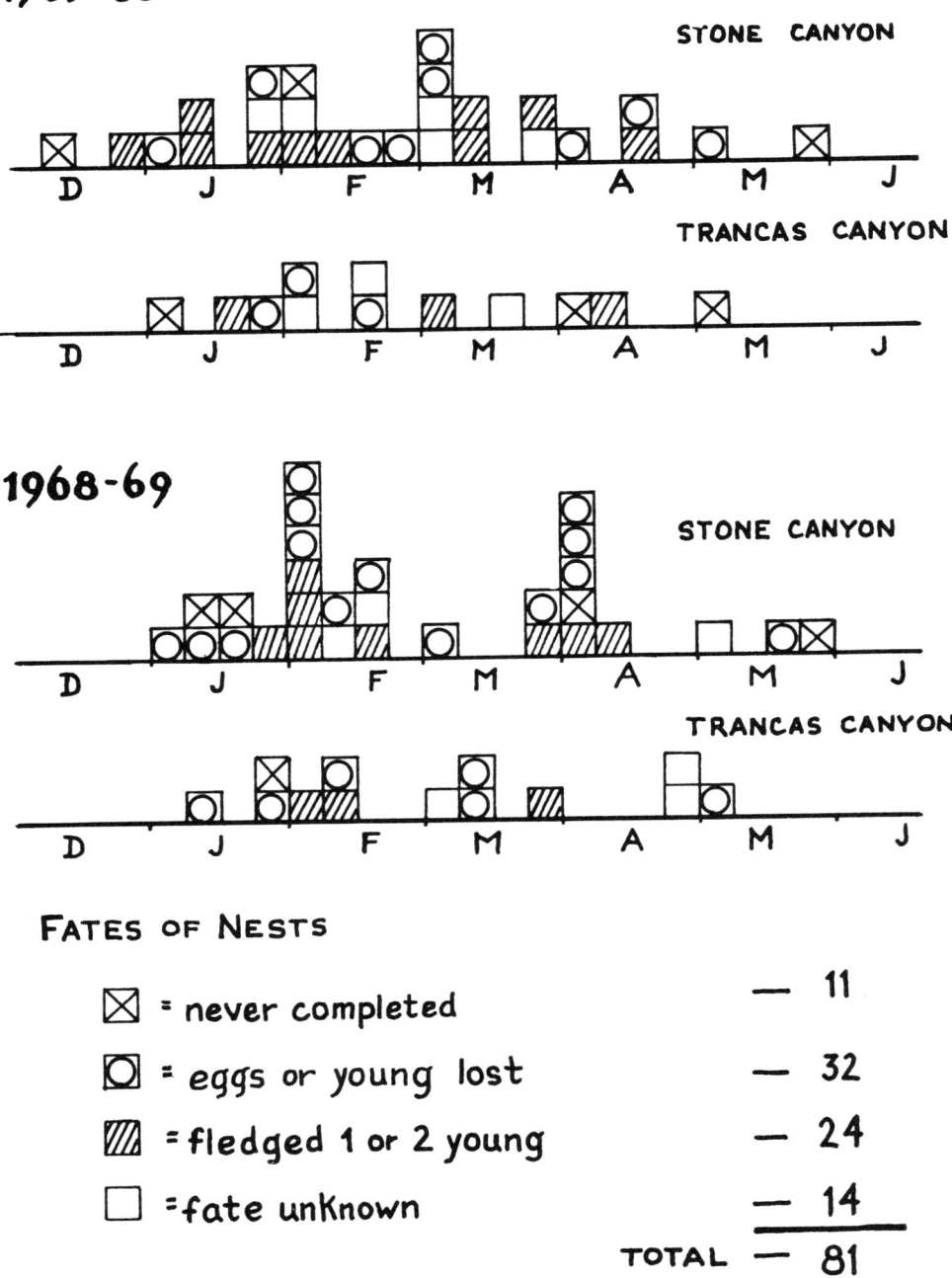

Fig. 6. Estimated dates of start of construction, and probable fates of *Calypte anna* nests found at Stone and Trancas Canyons during two breeding seasons.

(see fig. 6). Most females that started nesting in December through early February fledged young sometime in March, if the nesting was successful. These individuals began to renest in late March and April, the second nest usually being within a short distance of the first.

Ribes speciosum reached its peak of flowering in March (table 3; fig. 5), at which time it was an important food plant for nesting female *anna* in reasonably undisturbed canyons like Trancas, as well as for males in the hillside chaparral. By late March and early April, *Ribes* was declining but *Diplacus longiflorus*, *Salvia mellifera*, and *Nicotiana glauca* were starting to bloom vigorously in the chaparral. By mid- to late April, other hummingbird food plants like *Salvia spathacea* and *Silene laciniata* were blooming in oak woodlands, as at Trancas Canyon. The main floral food sources of breeding *anna* females in the Stone Canyon gardens were *Abutilon*, *Strelitzia*, and *Fuchsia*. *Eucalyptus* was important early in the breeding season, but its flowering had declined greatly by February; at this time, *Nicotiana* was increasing rapidly in blooming (fig. 3 and 5).

Juvenile *anna* were first seen in February, and had become locally common in chaparral areas by mid-March; their numbers continued to increase through most of April. Spring migrant *Selasphorus rufus* and *Calypte costae* arrived in the Santa Monica Mountains in early to mid-March. In the chaparral areas I studied, *rufus* never reached the numbers seen in the previous year; the greatest number recorded along the Franklin Canyon hilltop trail was 12. Migrant *rufus* left the study area by mid-April (see table 3; fig. 5).

Calypte costae was present on the Franklin Canyon study area in small numbers through most of March. However, even after reaching its greatest density in late March and April, *costae* was much less numerous than *anna*. The other breeding species, the Black-chinned Hummingbird, was first recorded in the Franklin Canyon chaparral on 7 April. Male *alexandri* were common in the chaparral by the sixteenth, and by May were nearly as abundant as *anna* had been two months earlier.

In early April many *anna* males began to show signs of body molt. Several color-marked males started losing their markings, and a number of birds had begun to appear decidedly scruffy on the back and sides. Also at about this time, I began seeing aberrant, incomplete display dives from several males, though not necessarily the same individuals that were starting to molt. By mid-April, most *anna* males were abandoning all or parts of their breeding territories, or were defending only a few of the richest food sources therein. By 1 May, only 2 or 3 males on the Franklin Canyon trail were still showing signs of full breeding territoriality. *Nicotiana* was the main food supply of most of these males, *Ribes* being almost through blooming. By 10 May, the last *anna* male had definitely left his breeding territory, and all individuals seen were in heavy molt, usually keeping to thick shrubbery and avoiding aggressive encounters. Song and display had practically ceased.

By mid-April, *anna* nesting activity was definitely on the wane in all areas studied. The latest clutches of eggs recorded were laid about 20 April (Trancas Canyon) and 5 May (Stone Canyon). I observed nest-building activity as late as 10 May at Stone and 25 May at Trancas, but these nests were apparently never completed. The latest successful *anna* nests in both areas were started in mid-April, and fledged young during the first week of June (table 3; fig. 6). In all, I found 27 *anna* nests at Stone Canyon and 12 at Trancas during 1967-68 (see fig. 6).

Black-chinned Hummingbirds began nesting activity at Stone and Trancas Canyons in late April, and the first known clutches of eggs were laid around 24-25 April (table 3). In all, I found 4 nests of *alexandri* at Trancas Canyon and 15 at Stone Canyon. The first *alexandri* fledglings were seen on 25 June at Trancas, and 15 July at Stone (table 3), where most of the early nests failed due to predation by orioles (see below). During the latter part of the *anna* nesting season and through that of *alexandri*, there was a wide variety of cultivated flowers available to hummingbirds (fig. 4). These included, in addition to *Abutilon* and *Strelitzia*, such shrubs as *Jacobinia*, *Callistemon*, *Melianthus*, *Cuphea ignea*, and *Hamelia patens*, and such herbs as *Heuchera* and *Impatiens*. In the adjacent chaparral and disturbed areas, *Salvia* and *Diplacus* abounded, and *Nicotiana* was still in good bloom.

Postbreeding season.—Soon after abandoning their breeding territories in April and early May, many adult male *anna* left the chaparral. By late May, few adult males remained in the chaparral, and many had moved into gardens and set up feeding territories at patches of cultivated flowers; others presumably left for the high mountains. Juvenile *anna* were also beginning to decline in numbers in chaparral areas at this time, but adult male *costae* and *alexandri* were still on breeding territories and juveniles of the former were becoming abundant (table 3). Many postbreeding Allen Hummingbirds, *Selasphorus sasin*, arrived in the Santa Monica Mountains in late May. By early June, they had taken over most of the *Nicotiana* stands on the coastal slope of the mountains. Adult *sasin* were not seen after mid-June, but juvenile *Selasphorus* were still abundant when observations were concluded in late July.

During April and early May, as *anna* males were leaving their breeding territories, *Diplacus*, *Salvia*, *Scrophularia*, and *Nicotiana* were in very good bloom. By late May, the first three had declined greatly but *Penstemon cordifolius* was flowering vigorously. *Penstemon* reached full bloom in June (fig. 5) and its flowering then declined rapidly. By mid-July, *Nicotiana* was the only important hummingbird food plant in and around chaparral areas.

Fig. 7. Hummingbird activity and blooming of chaparral food plants at Franklin Canyon, September 1968 through June 1969. See fig. 5 for derivations of graphs and abbreviations.

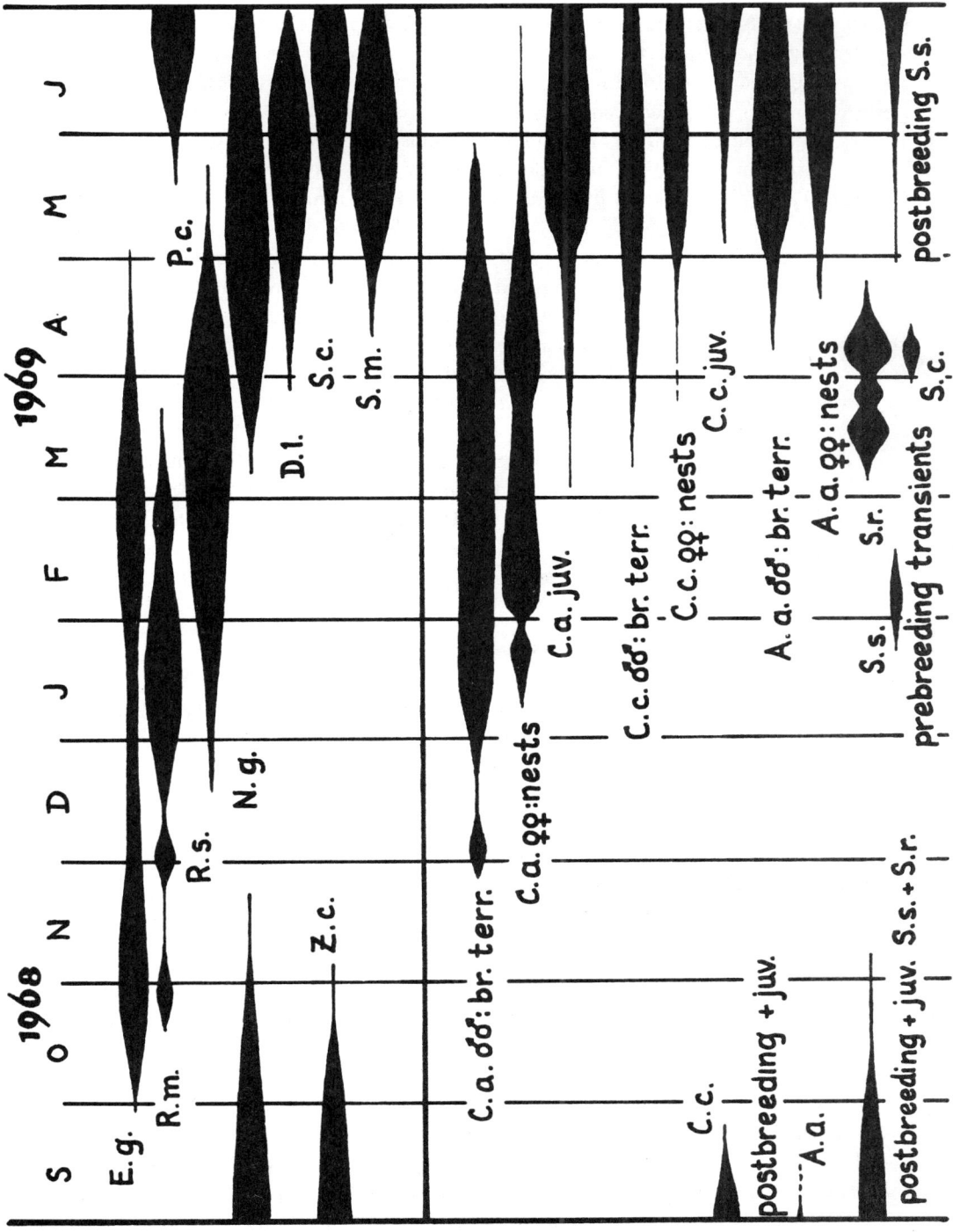

Through early and mid-June, breeding territoriality of *alexandri* males waned rapidly. By the end of the month, both they and *anna* juveniles had almost entirely deserted the chaparral and were now found in gardens, *Nicotiana* stands, or (presumably) in the high mountains. Male *costae* went off breeding territory in late June and early July, and all individuals seen thereafter were in heavy molt. During most of July, juvenile *costae* and *sasin* were practically the only hummers present in large numbers, and they were almost entirely restricted to stands of *Nicotiana*. After mid-July, a few *alexandri* juveniles also began to appear at *Nicotiana*, but by the end of July their numbers were still small.

In the oak woodlands and gardens, adult female *anna* began to decline in numbers about mid-May. By early June only a few individuals remained, mostly those still engaged in nesting; presumably the others had left for the high mountains. All through June, there was considerable Black-chin nesting activity, but during July the numbers of *alexandri* females also declined greatly. The latest *alexandri* nest I had under observation fledged young on 25 July. By the end of July, the commonest occupants of gardens like that at Stone Canyon were juvenile male *anna*. These and adult male *anna* held feeding territories at most of the good patches of flowers; juvenile *alexandri* and other *anna* were the commonest poachers. *Selasphorus* juveniles were common around the edges of the garden, mostly at *Nicotiana*.

1968-69 OBSERVATIONS

Observations during 1968-69 ran from 20 September 1968 to 6 June 1969, thereby including the entire prebreeding and breeding seasons, but only the beginning of the post-breeding season. Quantitative records of hummingbird activity were kept by means of trail censuses (fig. 9) and reservoir censuses (table 6) at the Franklin Canyon study area. Blooming seasons of chaparral food plants, in relation to hummingbird activity, are shown in figure 7. Dates and probable fates of *anna* nests at Stone and Trancas Canyons are given by figure 6. Data on molt, testis size, and territorial status of male *anna* collected during the prebreeding and early breeding season are presented in figure 8.

Prebreeding season.—During late September and October, *Nicotiana* provided the only important food source for hummingbirds in and around chaparral areas. The only native food plant in bloom was *Zauschneria*, which was visited mostly by small numbers of female and juvenile *anna*. Many *anna* males held feeding territories at cultivated flowers in shaded gardens like Stone Canyon.

As in the previous year, the numbers of *anna* at *Nicotiana* increased during October (table 6). After mid-October, flowering activity of *Nicotiana* and *Zauschneria* began to wane rapidly, and by early November had practically ceased.

Birds which had been visiting *Nicotiana* (and *Zauschneria*) had mostly moved to gardens or *Eucalyptus* groves by late October. In some areas, such as Malibu

Creek, *Eucalyptus globulus* began to flower early in October, and bloomed vigorously for several months. At Franklin and Stone Canyons (and in the eastern part of the mountains generally), *Eucalyptus* bloomed only weakly and sporadically, and was much less important as a hummingbird food source than in the previous year. The major floral food sources for *anna* in gardens during the fall were *Abutilon, Cestrum, Callistemon, Erythrina* spp., *Fuchsia, Hibiscus,* and *Strelitzia.*

Through almost all of October, November, and December the weather stayed hot and dry, with periodic showers and thunderstorms. Small amounts of rain (12 mm. or less) fell on several occasions (fig. 12), and each of these rainy periods was accompanied by a few days of cool weather.

After the showers of mid-October, some *Ribes malvaceum* began to put out leaves and even flowers, but these were almost entirely ignored by hummingbirds except for a few female *anna*. The brief spell of cool weather and showers

TABLE 6

MOVEMENTS OF ANNA HUMMINGBIRDS BETWEEN DIFFERENT HABITATS AND FOOD PLANTS: RESERVOIR CENSUSES, FRANKLIN CANYON, 1968-69

Location of *C. anna*, irrespective of age or sex	Dates of censuses														
	10 Oct.	12 Nov.	1 Dec.	14 Dec.	30 Dec.	13 Jan.	1 Feb.	22 Feb.	15 March	1 April	10 April	23 April	5 May	22 May	6 June
Habitat															
Chaparral	0	2	13	3	12	19	26	31	31	27	29	17	9	3	3
Nicotiana scrub	10	8	3	1	0	0	0	0	0	0	0	5	7	8	6
Woodlands, groves	2	1	2	2	3	5	4	7	9	11	10	3	4	3	2
Gardens, orchards	5	4	4	11	7	6	7	9	9	8	13	18	16	15	16
Food plant															
Nicotiana glauca	10	4	2	1	-	-	-	-	-	-	2	8	11	7	6
Eucalyptus globulus	2	3	2	1	2	-	-	-	-	-	-	-	-	-	-
Citrus orchard	-	-	1	5	3	4	3	3	5	4	10	11	6	7	5
Cultivated flowers	4	4	5	7	4	2	5	6	4	6	4	7	10	8	14
Zauschneria spp.	2	1	0	-	-	-	-	-	-	-	-	-	-	-	-
Ribes malvaceum	0	3	11	3	10	12	10	3	1	-	-	-	-	-	-
Ribes speciosum	-	-	-	-	-	9	14	20	25	24	21	16	5	1	-
Diplacus longiflorus	-	-	-	-	-	-	-	-	-	-	-	-	2	5	5
Salvia mellifera	-	-	-	-	-	-	-	-	-	-	-	-	1	2	1
Penstemon cordifolius	-	-	-	-	-	-	-	-	-	-	-	-	-	-	3
Number of males with feeding territories	10	9	3	12	6	4	2	2	1	0	2	8	7	8	7
Number of males with breeding territories	0	0	11	2	8	16	25	30	31	28	27	17	8	3	0
Total number of *C. anna* recorded on census	17	17	22	17	22	30	37	47	49	46	52	43	36	29	27

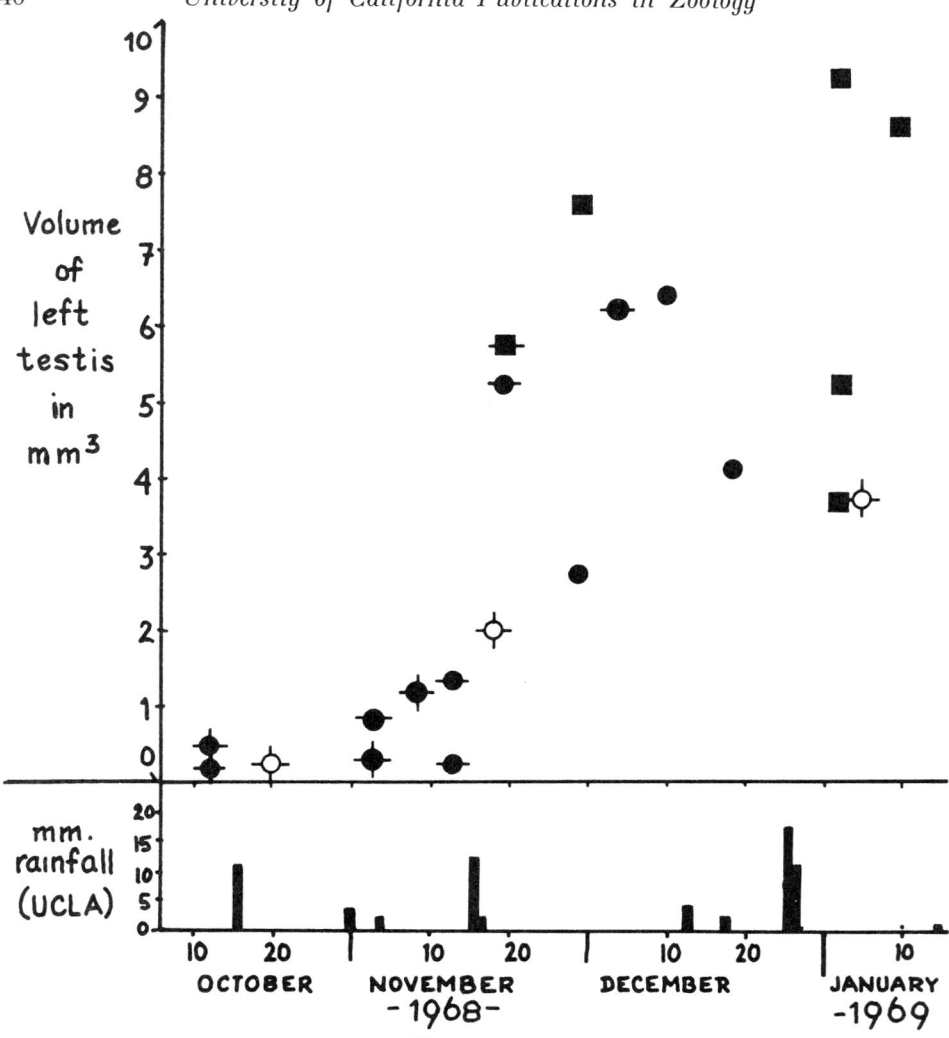

Fig. 8. Testis volume, molt, and territorial status of male *C. anna* collected in the Santa Monica Mountains during fall and winter, 1968-69.
Testis volumes calculated from the formula V = 4/3 a b², where a = testis width and b = testes length (see Williamson, 1956).

in mid-November triggered another, larger burst of flowering in *Ribes malvaceum* (fig. 5). This time, a number of males moved out into the chaparral and began to set up breeding territories, both at Stone and Franklin Canyons (see table 6). After these rains, all adult male *anna* collected had enlarged testes (fig. 8). However, during late November and early December hot, dry weather returned; by 10 December, *Ribes* blooming activity had again subsided and nearly all *anna* males had moved back onto feeding territories in gardens and *Eucalyptus* groves. At this time, all adult male *anna* collected had completed the annual molt (fig. 8).

There was a cold, wet spell in mid-December and although very little rain actually fell, there was a brief but distinct resurgence of song and display activity among male *anna*. Female *anna*, which had been slowly increasing in gardens and oak woodlands through November and December, began to show some preliminary signs of nesting at this time (see below). However, I saw no birds actually gathering nesting material, and doubt that any nests were started. By 20 December, the weather was again hot and dry and no further signs of breeding activity were seen.

The first heavy winter rains and the first prolonged period of cool weather came on the 25-26 December. By the thirtieth *Ribes malvaceum* showed a strong resurgence of flowering, and *anna* males were again moving out into the chaparral and setting up what this time proved to be the definitive breeding territories. Female *anna* moved into good feeding areas in gardens and oak woodlands, and commenced nesting activity early in January. Until *Ribes malvaceum* began to bloom, there had been very little hummingbird activity of any kind in oak woodland sites like Trancas Canyon.

Breeding season.—Flowering activity of *Ribes malvaceum* peaked around mid-January. At full bloom, *malvaceum* had considerably fewer flowers than in the previous year, as many bushes which started to bloom in October and November did not flower at all in January. *Ribes speciosum* began to bloom in early January, and by the end of the month it was already of greater importance to hummingbirds than was *malvaceum* (fig. 7). Numbers of territorial male *anna* in the chaparral increased rapidly in early January, leveled off briefly, then climbed rapidly again as *speciosum* came into good bloom (fig. 12). Only a few additional birds obtained territories in February, and the number of *anna* males holding breeding territories reached its maximum early in the month (fig. 9, table 6).

In late January and early February, a few spring migrant *Selasphorus sasin* were seen in the chaparral at Franklin and Trancas Canyons. None of this species were recorded in chaparral areas during the previous spring, perhaps because of the fact that *Eucalyptus* was in much better bloom in the Los Angeles Basin in 1968 than in 1969.

The first nest-building activity by female *anna* was seen on 3 January at Stone Canyon and 10 January at Trancas. The first recorded clutches of eggs were completed around 18-20 January in both areas (table 3). A major interruption in

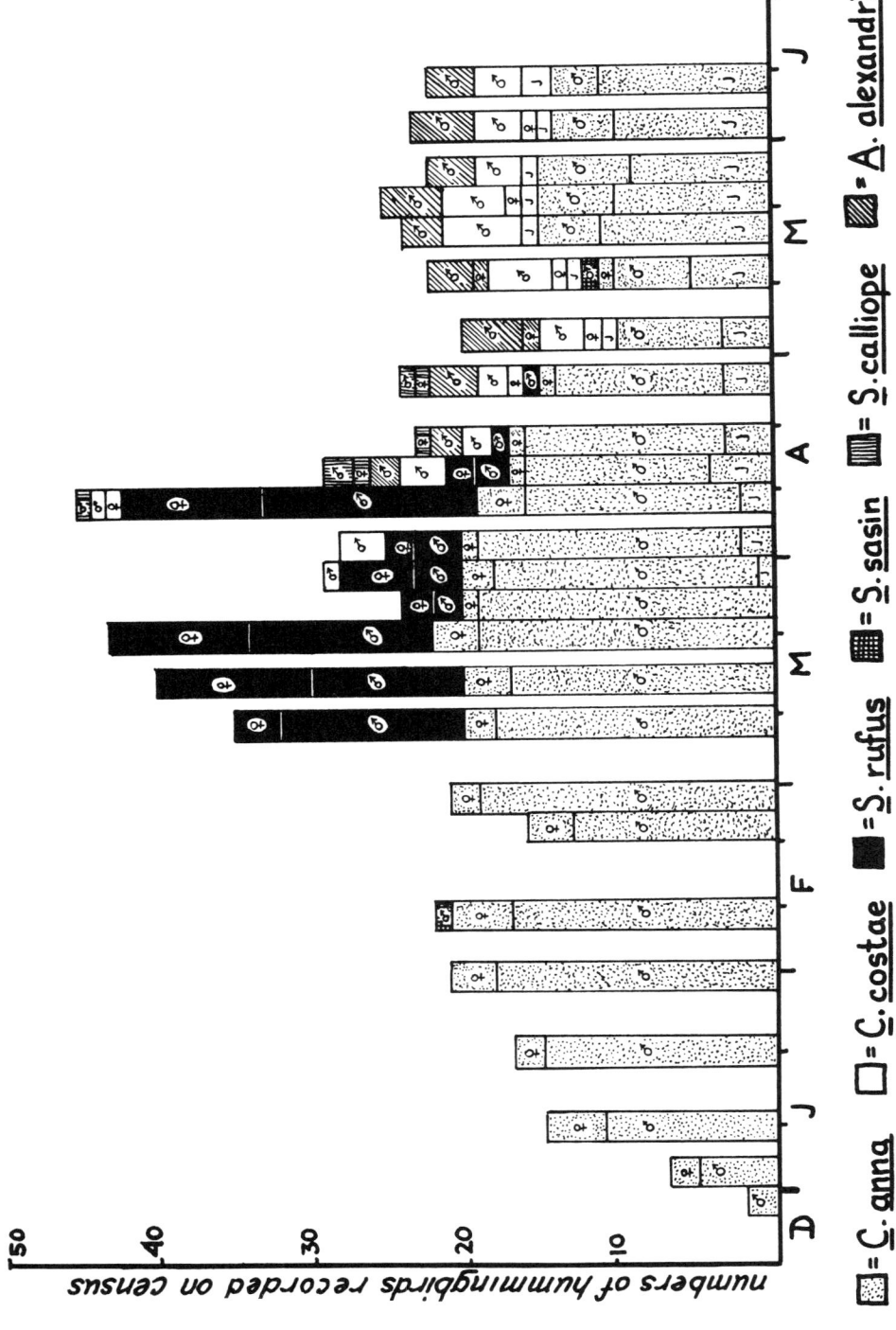

nesting occurred in late January, in the form of extraordinarily heavy and violent rains. From the nineteenth through the twenty-sixth, at least one inch of rain fell every day except the twenty-third, with over 4 inches on the twentieth and twenty-fifth (figs. 1, 12). This rain caused floods and landslides all through the Los Angeles area, and turned Trancas Creek into a raging torrent. It was mid-February before I could get across the creek to census the oak woodland on the far side!

All of the early nests at Stone and Trancas were destroyed or abandoned by 1 February, presumably on account of the rains. Following the deluge, there was an enormous surge of nest-building activity in both areas during the first half of February (fig. 6), presumably involving females who had lost nests in the rain as well as those who had not nested before. The rains apparently had little or no effect on the flowering of *Ribes*, or on male breeding territoriality. However, blooming of many cultivated flowers was notably retarded (see fig. 4), and flowering activity remained rather low in Stone Canyon during February. Only *Cestrum*, *Abutilon*, and *Strelitzia* were in good bloom, and there were frequent disputes between female *anna* over feeding rights. These altercations soon subsided as eggs were laid and incubation progressed in most of the nests. In the successful nests at Stone Canyon, eggs hatched in late February or early March and young fledged between 12 and 31 March. Since a high proportion of these nests were indeed successful, much of the female *anna* population remained fairly synchronized, starting nests for their second broods within a two-week span around the beginning of April. Due at least in part to more nest failures, the Trancas population showed less synchrony (fig. 6).

The timing of arrival of spring migrant *rufus*, *costae*, and *alexandri* in 1969 was fairly similar to that in 1968 (table 3). Migrant *rufus* entered the chaparral in numbers as large as those seen in 1967, perhaps reflecting the aforementioned scarcity of blooming *Eucalyptus* in the area. Several large waves of *rufus* passed through the Franklin Canyon chaparral in March and early April, and exerted a considerable disruptive effect on breeding territoriality of adult male *anna* (see below). By 10 April, the last major *rufus* wave had passed, and male *anna* were again vigorously territorial (figs. 9, 13). At Stone Canyon, migrant *rufus* were seen mostly in the chaparral and the *Eucalyptus* grove; they did not penetrate the garden grove where most female *anna* were nesting.

Numbers of *alexandri* males increased rapidly in mid- to late April, and the first *alexandri* nesting activity was noted about this time. The first recorded *alexandri* clutches were completed around 20 and 28 April at Stone and Trancas Canyons, respectively. From late March on, *costae* males held breeding territories in chaparral areas, but never in large numbers. I found two *costae* nests in May

---

Fig. 9. Numbers of hummingbirds recorded on censuses along the ridgetop trail at Franklin Canyon during winter and spring, 1968-69.

at Trancas Canyon; the clutches were probably completed around 10-15 April and 15-20 May.

In contrast to the spring migrants, the arrival of juvenile *anna* in the chaparral was over a month later than in previous years (table 3). Local concentrations appeared at good feeding areas by mid-April, and during late April and May juvenile *anna* numbers rose sharply (fig. 9).

The first signs of molt in *anna* males were noted about 10 April, slightly later than in 1968. Along the ridgetop trail at Franklin Canyon, the number of territorial males declined sharply in mid-April (figs. 9, 13). No further marked decreases in number of males on breeding territories was noted until mid-May, but there was an apparent turnover in individuals (fig. 6). Of the 4 territorial males on 10 May, only 1 or 2 had held the same territories a month before. The others were occupying sites or perches not used earlier in the season, and demonstrated some of the behavioral signs of being recently established, for example advertising flights (see below). I strongly suspect that these were individuals that had previously been prevented from establishing territories by the original residents.

By early May, most *anna* males seen were in heavy body molt. All birds still holding breeding territories at this time had shifted their feeding activities to *Nicotiana*; from early May on, aberrant, incomplete display flights were common. The last *anna* males gradually abandoned their breeding territories in late May (fig. 13; table 6).

Stone and Trancas Canyons each held 3 active *anna* nests by early May. The latest recorded *anna* clutch was completed on 22 May, but this nest later failed. When observations were concluded in early June, several nests still had young. At this time, nests of *alexandri* in all stages were present at Stone and Trancas. Postbreeding *anna* males and juvenile *anna* were now beginning to invade the gardens at Stone, establishing feeding territories at such plants as *Abutilon*, *Fuchsia*, and *Cestrum*.

Postbreeding season.—Events of the early postbreeding season are best illustrated by the reservoir censuses (table 6). A decrease in numbers of *anna* males holding breeding territories in the chaparral was at first accompanied by a corresponding increase in birds on feeding territories in gardens and the citrus grove. However, total numbers of *anna* recorded in the censuses declined continuously from mid-April on. Most of this decline was accounted for by adult males; juveniles increased until late May. This probably does represent an actual exodus of adults from the study area, most likely to the high mountains.

As of 6 June, postbreeding *Selasphorus* and *costae* juveniles had not yet appeared in the Santa Monica Mountains area in numbers, although a single adult male *sasin* was seen on several occasions in April and early May. *Nicotiana* stands in many parts of the mountains were utilized almost exclusively by *alexandri*. Particularly at dawn and dusk, small numbers of *anna* juveniles also visited *Nicotiana*.

1969-70 OBSERVATIONS

During 1969-70 I was unable to be in the field continuously, and my observations are thus somewhat fragmentary. Between 16 October and 16 December, I tried to obtain more information on initiation of breeding in the Anna Hummingbird, to compare with data from previous years (see fig. 12). Table 7 summarizes the shifts between different food plants of *anna* at Stone Canyon during this period. Further observations were made 6 January-21 February and 12 April-27 June 1970, to obtain comparative data on timing of other events of the annual cycle (table 3).

Prebreeding season.—In mid-October, *Nicotiana* was in poor bloom in the Santa Monica Mountains, and supported very few territorial birds (mostly first-year male *anna*). *Zauschneria*, still blooming in a few canyon bottoms, was visited by small numbers of female *anna*.

The major hummingbird food plants at Stone Canyon in mid-October were *Fuchsia, Abutilon, Heliconia,* and *Hibiscus*. The *Eucalyptus* grove was just coming into bloom, and as its flowering increased it became the major focus of hummingbird activity through December. The blooming of *Abutilon, Fuchsia,* and *Heliconia* declined at this time but that of *Strelitzia* increased, also reflected in their utilization by hummingbirds (table 7).

Breeding reason.—The first significant winter rains fell on 6 November (fig. 12); although there had been a few very local thunderstorms in October, the weather was generally hot and dry. Immediately following this rain, there was a great increase in activity by male *anna* in chaparral areas. Display dives were seen, chases increased, and a few birds appeared to be setting up breeding territories in chaparral adjacent to blooming *Eucalyptus* (table 7).

By mid-November, *Ribes malvaceum* was beginning to bloom in the chaparral, and the number of males holding breeding territories was increasing rapidly. Interestingly, many of these males showed in varying degree certain behavior patterns I associate with feeding territoriality: perching inconspicuously inside shrubs, chipping rather than singing at the approach of an intruder, etc. Also, a number of these birds had not yet completed the molt of the crown and gorget. However, by late November virtually all birds were through molting and showed full breeding territoriality. By mid-December, the numbers of male *anna* on breeding territories were approaching the peak numbers recorded in other years in most areas. *Ribes malvaceum* was approaching full bloom at this time, and *Ribes speciosum* was starting to flower.

A female *anna* was seen gathering nesting material on 6 December at Franklin Canyon, and on the sixteenth I found a nearly completed nest at Stone Canyon. On 19 January I observed a recently fledged juvenile at Stone Canyon. Assuming that the bird had fledged around 15 January, the date of egglaying would prob-

TABLE 7

Food Plant Utilization by Anna Hummingbirds at Stone Canyon,
Censuses of October 1969 through February 1970
Dates Given as in Table 3.

Food Plant	Date of census								
	X:18	X:27	XI:7	XI:22	XII:3	XII:16	I:19	II:6	II:20
Cultivated									
Abutilon hybrids	4	4	5	4	2	2	2	3	3
Cestrum elegans	3	1	2	3	3	2	3	3	3
Fuchsia spp. & hybrids	6	9	4	2	3	3	1	2	4
Heliconia hybrids	5	5	2	1	2	1	1	1	0
Hibiscus rosa-sinensis	5	5	3	3	3	3	2	2	7
Strelitzia reginae	2	3	2	2	3	3	2	4	4
Other	3	2	1	3	4	5	5	2	5
Naturalized									
Eucalyptus globulus	7	13	27	30	24	21	27	18	16
Nicotiana glauca	5	3	1	0	0	0	0	0	0
Native									
Ribes malvaceum	0	0	0	5	7	14	4	3	0
Ribes speciosum	0	0	0	0	0	0	1	14	24
Totals									
Males with feeding territories	12	15	14	11	4	5	8	5	3
Males with breeding territories	0	0	1?	6	11	14	7	12	12
Females	9	11	12	13	15	15	14	15	16
Juveniles	0	0	0	0	0	0	1	3	8

ably be around 5-10 December; nest-building probably began in the last week of November.

Between 10 November 1969 and 9 January 1970, no rain fell and the weather became increasingly hot and dry. The blooming of both *Ribes* species was greatly curtailed, and a number of *anna* males abandoned their breeding territories in the chaparral. Some birds returned to feeding territories at *Eucalyptus* or cultivated flowers, and most birds that continued to hold breeding territories were forced to commute to feeding areas elsewhere, usually at *Eucalyptus* (see table 8). I have no data on the effects of this pronounced dry spell upon the nesting of female *anna*. However, to judge from the numbers of juvenile *anna* in the chaparral by mid-April, nesting success could not have been greatly impaired.

Between 9 and 16 January some 65 millimeters of rain fell, mostly on the eleventh and sixteenth. The recovery of *Ribes* was slow, but by early to mid-February, *speciosum* was blooming vigorously. The number of territorial male *anna* along the ridgetop at Franklin Canyon increased from 6 on 13 January to 13 by 20 February. At Stone Canyon, there was an almost immediate movement out into the chaparral, accompanied by a drop in the number of males on feeding territories at *Eucalyptus*. However, until *Ribes* began to bloom strongly, many chaparral males commuted to the *Eucalyptus* grove to feed (table 7).

At least 7 or 8 *anna* nests were begun in late January and early February. Several of these were in the immediate vicinity of the *Eucalyptus* grove, which continued to be a major focus of hummingbird activity through most of February. Besides *Eucalyptus*, the major food plants utilized by nesting females during this period were *Abutilon*, *Aloe*, *Hibiscus*, and *Strelitzia*. By late February, the *Fuchsia* in the garden grove was blooming, and *Aloe* and *Eucalyptus* were declining.

The mid-January rains proved to be the last of the entire breeding season; the winter and spring of 1969-70 were the driest in the history of the UCLA weather station. By the time observations were resumed in April, the chaparral was extremely dry, and many adult male *anna* were leaving their breeding territories. *Ribes speciosum* had all but finished flowering, though *Diplacus*, *Salvia*, and *Nicotiana* were in good bloom. Juvenile *anna* were numerous in the chaparral, and several *Selasphorus rufus*, doubtless prebreeding migrants, were still present. By early May, all *anna* males had abandoned their breeding territories, and nesting activity by female *anna* ended soon thereafter—considerably earlier than in the two previous years (table 3).

Postbreeding season.—The weather remained hot and dry through late June, by which time the chaparral had reached a state of desiccation not normally seen until late July or August. *Salvia* and *Diplacus* reached full bloom in early May and had nearly ceased flowering by late June. *Nicotiana* reached a peak of flowering by late June, but certain other hummingbird food plants, notably *Penstemon* and *Scrophularia*, scarcely bloomed at all, presumably due to the exceptional dryness.

Juvenile *anna* remained common in the Franklin Canyon chaparral through mid-May, but by June few were seen. Males of *costae* and *alexandri* held breeding territories through mid-June. Juvenile *costae*, though not so numerous as in previous years, were still common in the chaparral in late June, by which time a few postbreeding *Selasphorus* had appeared at stands of *Nicotiana* (table 3).

No nesting activity of *anna* or *alexandri* was found at Trancas Canyon in late spring; indeed, from late April on only *costae* were seen there. Trancas Creek was entirely dry and the blooming of several food plants (*Salvia spathacea*, *Diplacus*, *Silene*) was greatly curtailed. At Stone and lower Franklin Canyons *alexandri* nested at about the same time as in previous years (table 3), but the number of nests found at the latter locality was far larger than in any previous season. Nesting success of these Franklin Canyon birds is presented in table 11.

Feeding Territoriality in the Prebreeding Season

During the heat of summer, most *anna* activity in the lowlands is concentrated in shady gardens and other planted areas. Through much of October, there is a decided increase in numbers of *anna* males holding feeding territories at *Nicotiana*. Although there is probably some movement out of the gardens at this time, most of this increase probably reflects the return of birds from their summer sojourn in the high mountains.

The buildup in *anna* numbers at *Nicotiana* usually follows fairly closely upon the departure of postbreeding *Selasphorus*. I cannot state whether the *Selasphorus* leave because of increased competition from the augmented numbers of *anna*, or whether *anna* move into *Nicotiana* only after the *Selasphorus* have abandoned it. A possible slight time lag between the departure of *Selasphorus* and attainment of maximum *anna* numbers at *Nicotiana* (table 5) may provide some support for the latter alternative. In most years, *Nicotiana* reaches a peak of flowering in September, then declines through October and finally ceases to bloom in November. By this time, *Eucalyptus* is beginning to bloom in some years, and a marked shift of *anna* feeding activity to this food source occurs. In those years when *Eucalyptus* does not bloom strongly, male anna usually move into gardens and plantings (see tables 6, 7).

Both adult and first-year males hold feeding territories at *Nicotiana*, *Eucalyptus*, or other rich, localized food sources during the prebreeding season. First-year males, the young of the previous breeding season now well into the postjuvenal molt, tend to be subordinate to older males; they often occupy smaller territories, containing fewer flowers. When a food source begins to decline, as does *Nicotiana* during October in most years, adult males often abandon their feeding territories and move elsewhere rather quickly, while some first-year males remain until there are practically no flowers left (cf. table 5). The postjuvenal molt is apparently very protracted in some birds (or perhaps these are the young of very late broods). Some individuals may retain juvenile (white-tipped) rectrices and incomplete red crowns and gorgets until well into the breeding season (cf. fig. 8). Most individuals, however, appear to attain full adult plumage by about mid-January (cf. Williamson, 1956).

Female *anna* are practically always decidedly subordinate to males during the prebreeding season (it is usually not possible to distinguish first-year from older females at this time). Females do not appear to hold feeding territories during the prebreeding season, but visit flowers not being defended by territorial birds, or try to poach off the feeding territories of males. When no territorial birds are present, female *anna* manifest considerable intolerance of one another at flowers. However, this aggressiveness is usually confined to chattering and other threat behavior, and is rarely consistent enough or localized enough to warrant being called territoriality. During the fall months at Stone Canyon, several female *anna* appeared to spend most of their time foraging for insects in the tops of oak and alder trees of the garden grove. Periodically these individuals would fly down and attempt to forage at the various flowers in the gardens, most of which were defended by territorial male *anna*. Very small numbers of female *anna* were seen away from gardens, *Nicotiana*, or other flowers during October and November. These birds were usually found in riparian woodlands, and appeared to be living entirely upon insects.

Among the cultivated flowers that supported feeding territories of *anna* males during the prebreeding season may be mentioned *Abutilon*, *Cestrum*, *Fuchsia*, *Heliconia*, and *Hibiscus*, all of which secrete copious nectar (cf. table 1). One rich nectar source that was used frequently by female *anna* but never appeared to support territorial males was *Strelitzia*. I do not know the reason for this; perhaps the rather complex floral morphology (cf. Skead, 1967) plays some role here, although the bills of male and female *anna* are practically the same length (table 2).

Breeding Territoriality of Male Anna Hummingbirds

A breeding territory requires much more time and energy to maintain than does a feeding territory (Stiles, 1971a): a larger area is defended, chases are longer and more frequent, display dives are given, and song is more presistent. A male on breeding territory therefore requires a food source that is rich, dependable, and easily exploited in order to maintain a vigorous and consistent defense. Flowers can be much more efficiently exploited as a food resource than can insects; they are stationary and conspicuous, requiring minimal time and energy to find and "pursue." Flower nectar, being essentially pure carbohydrate and water (Percival, 1961), is almost 100 percent assimilable. Thus, access to a rich nectar source is very important for a breeding male *anna*. The most important food flowers of *anna* on breeding territories in the Santa Monica Mountains are the two species of *Ribes* and *Eucalyptus globulus*. In the higher parts of the mountains *Arctostaphylos* spp. may be visited; where suitable breeding habitat is found adjacent to gardens or planted areas, a variety of cultivated flowers may be locally important. Late in the breeding season, some territorial *anna* males forage extensively at *Nicotiana*. However, in terms of amount of nectar per flower, number of flowers per plant, length of blooming season, and wide distribution in the area, *Ribes speciosum* can be most efficiently exploited of native food plants, and *Eucalyptus* of introduced ones (table 1).

In the Franklin Canyon chaparral, most *anna* males establish breeding territories with reference to a *Ribes* food source. The first males to take up territories occupy sites where *Ribes malvaceum* is flowering (cf. fig. 10), and these sites are occupied in roughly the same order as their *Ribes* comes into good bloom. During the initial phases of setting up breeding territories, boundary disputes

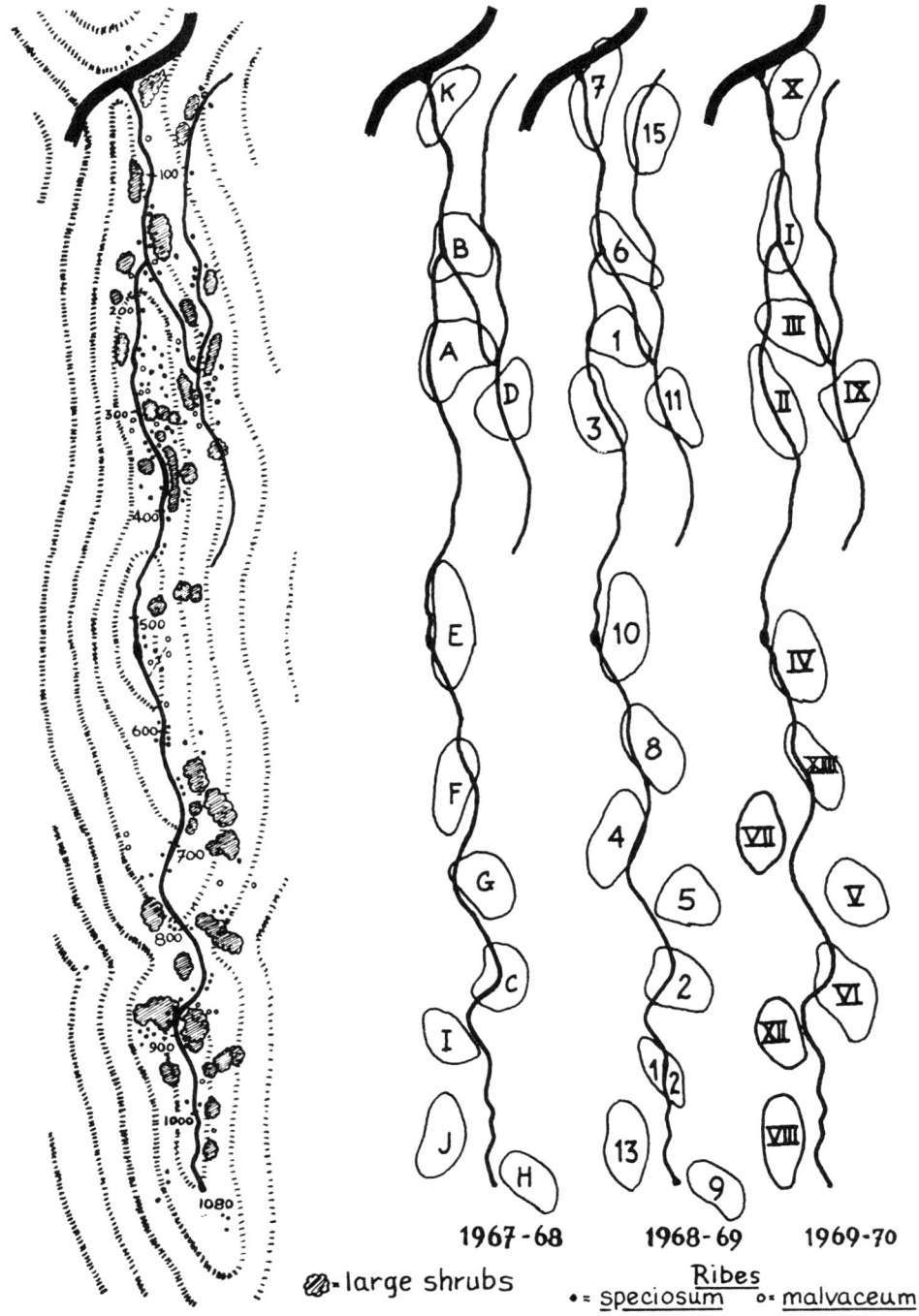

are frequent, and on several occasions I have seen two males singing furiously at one another from perches not over 10 feet apart. Advertising flights are also very frequent as territorial boundaries are being defined. Once boundaries have been established, these kinds of activities become very infrequent.

As *Ribes speciosum* replaces *R. malvaceum* as the main hummingbird food plant, established male *anna* may shift their territorial boundaries somewhat to compensate for the changes in food distribution. A few additional males may move into areas not previously occupied, and the maximum number and final distribution of territorial birds in any given area usually is a reflection of the distribution and abundance of *Ribes speciosum*. In the higher parts of the mountains, as at the Murphy Ranch, *Arctostaphylos* and *Ribes malvaceum* are the most important food plants in determining the distribution of *anna* breeding territories.

In setting up breeding territories, male *anna* usually occupy sites with a good *Ribes* supply first (fig. 10). The last birds into an area may be forced to hold territories at sites with little or no floral food supplies. These latter birds must commute between breeding territory and feeding area, often over considerable distances (see below). Sites with a copious *Ribes* supply are consistently occupied, year after year, whereas less favorable sites may not be (see fig. 10).

Flowering *Eucalyptus* trees are a staple food source of territorial male *anna* in areas where the *Eucalyptus* grows adjacent to suitable chaparral. In such a situation, one to several birds may defend breeding territories in the chaparral, and commute to the *Eucalyptus* several times an hour to feed. Each bird usually feeds in a different portion of the *Eucalyptus*, and although each is typically very aggressive toward intruders in his section when he is present at the tree, there is no consistent defense of the feeding area per se. The breeding *anna* males observed by Pitelka (1951) and Ortiz (1967) appeared to operate in this fashion. Ortiz describes a bird that made an average of three trips an hour between his breeding territory and a particular patch of flowers in the Berkeley Botanical Garden. The distance flown was about 800 meters each way, and the bird fed for just 20 to 80 seconds on each trip. I have records of *anna* males commuting to *Eucalyptus* trees to feed from distances of 50 to 700 meters at Stone Canyon (table 8), and up to 1 kilometer in other areas.

Obviously, these two patterns of food distribution in relation to territory location are not mutually exclusive—in fact, they represent the ends of a continuum. Many *anna* males observed in this study obtained part of their food on their

---

Fig. 10. The ridgetop study site at Franklin Canyon.
    Left: general map, showing distribution of *Ribes* and locations of large shrubs (which frequently serve to separate core areas of adjacent males). Distances along the ridgetop trail marked in meters.
    Right: locations of breeding territories (core areas) of male *anna* on 1 March 1968, 26 February 1969, and 21 February 1970, respectively. Territories are numbered or lettered in the order in which they were occupied in any given year.

TABLE 8

RELATION BETWEEN AMOUNT OF FOOD ON TERRITORY AND VISITATION OF OUTSIDE FOOD SOURCES
BY FOUR BREEDING MALE ANNA HUMMINGBIRDS:
STONE CANYON, 20 FEBRUARY 1970, 0900-1200

Male #	Amount of Ribes speciosum on territory		Outside food sources						Total no. trips	Total time off territory[2]
			Eucalyptus grove A		Eucalyptus grove B		Garden grove			
	No. bushes	Approx, no. flowers	Dist. from core area[1]	No. trips	Dist. from core area[1]	No. trips	Dist. from core area[1]	No. trips		
1	3	900	50	3,3?	500	1?	350	0	7	13:01
2	7	2000	120	2	650	0	250	1?	3	1:45
3	5	500	175	1,2 ?	700	0	200	5	8	13:56
4	3	250	200	2, 2?	550	4, 2?	300	0	10	20:35

1. Distance from center of core area, in meters.
2. Total time off territory, on flights known or suspected to have involved feeding at one of the three areas listed above. Times given as minutes: seconds.

territory from *Ribes* (or *Arctostaphylos*), and part from outside food sources to which they commuted. For 4 such males at Stone Canyon, the number of times per hour a male left his territory to feed (as well as the total time off territory) was inversely proportional to the amount of *Ribes* on his territory (table 8). And as *Ribes speciosum* increased in blooming activity at Stone Canyon, the number of times that different males left their territories to feed decreased, in some cases to zero (see above).

The amount of food on territory also appears to be related to the amount of time a male spends in territorial defense. I was able to verify this for *anna* males A and D (see fig. 10) at Franklin Canyon in 1968 (table 9). Male A controlled much more *Ribes* on his territory than did male D. At the same times of day and under very comparable weather conditions, male A spent almost twice as much time in territorial defense (see table 9).

The above observations strongly suggest that competition is more intense for those territories containing a food supply. This is borne out by the much more rapid and consistent replacement of males removed from such territories. A male removed from a territory containing little or no food may not be replaced at all.

Territory A at Franklin Canyon, an area with a notably rich *Ribes* supply (see fig. 10), was occupied by a marked *anna* male during spring 1968. I hap-

TABLE 9

RELATION BETWEEN AMOUNT OF FOOD ON TERRITORY AND AMOUNT OF TERRITORIAL DEFENSE
BY TWO MARKED MALE ANNA HUMMINGBIRDS:
FRANKLIN CANYON, FEBRUARY 1968.

Males: color mark and territory (see fig. 10)	White, A	Yellow, D
Number of flowering *Ribes speciosum* bushes on territory	ca. 55	ca. 15
Date & time (total 3 hours)	4 Feb., 1315-1615	22 Feb., 1300-1600
Weather and temperature range	Hazy sun, no breeze; 19-24°C	Hazy sun, slight breeze; 20-24°C
Chases (number, time spent)	14, 2?—7:26	9, 4?—2:54
Display dives (number of bouts, number of dives, time spent)	1, 2; 0:28	3, 6; 1:39
Total time spent in active territorial defense	7:54	4:33
Defenses against:		
male *anna*	4, 3?	3, 1?
female *anna*	3, 2?	1, 2?
juvenile *anna*	0	1, 1?
unidentified hummingbirds	4+	3+
nonhummingbirds	1	3, 1?

pened to be present on 26 February when this male left in a chase, and failed to return for several days. Within half an hour, an unmarked male was present on the territory (not one of the adjacent territorial males). Within two hours, this bird had transformed from a nervous, flighty intruder into an extremely pugnacious resident. He controlled the territory at least through 1 March, but by 3 March the original marked male was again in possession.

At the same site on 22 March 1969, *anna* male no. 1 was killed at dusk (see fig. 10). On the next day, 3 birds were contending for the territory—the 2 adjacent territorial males and a third, presumably without a territory of his own. By the afternoon of 26 March, this latter bird (no. 16) had established control over the area. Around 28-29 March, this bird sustained an injury and was unable to balance properly when perched. The bird rapidly became enfeebled, and disappeared between 10 and 15 April. His place was promptly taken by a third male (no. 21) who occupied this territory and part of the adjacent one until 20-25 April, by which time the *Ribes* there had nearly finished blooming (see fig. 11).

In the same two years, territories with little or no food thereon were apparently abandoned well before most *anna* males went off breeding territory, and were not reoccupied (or if so, only briefly). Examples include territories F, H, and K in 1968 and 4, 8, 12, 14, and 15 (figs. 6, 10) in 1969. Some of these sites were among the last to be occupied in that year; those occupied earlier usually contained *Ribes malvaceum* but relatively little *speciosum*.

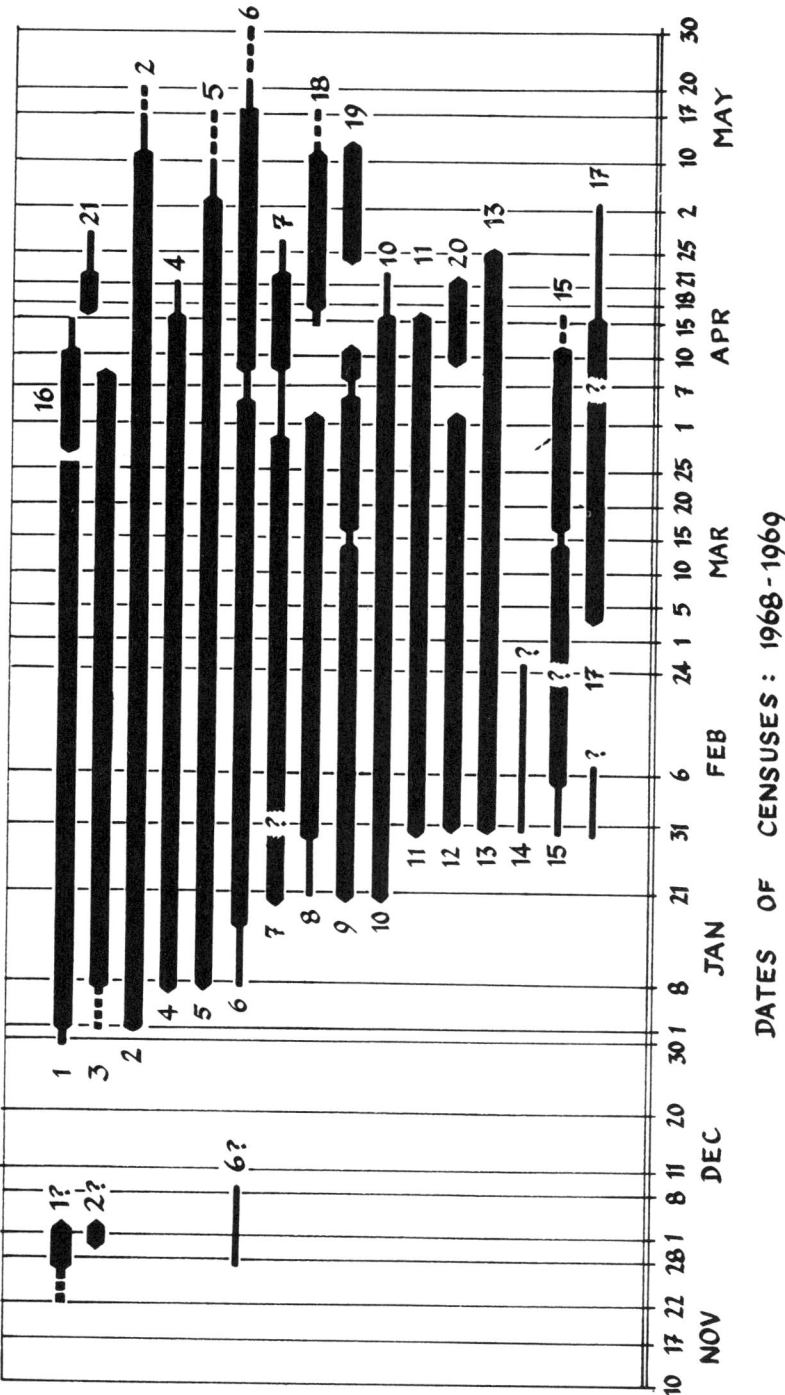

Males that must leave their territories to feed are at a further disadvantage in that they often must fly through or over the territories of other males in order to reach their food supply. The other males often attack and chase the bird in question, and if the hapless commuter must traverse several other territories, the respective males often subject him to a veritable gauntlet. One such bird in lower Franklin Canyon spent up to 7 minutes at a time off his territory when he flew to the orange grove to feed (ca. 400 m. away). When he returned, he was often chased by as many as 4 different males, sometimes for a considerable distance. I have noticed that when a 2-bird chase passes over the territory of an *anna* male, he almost invariably attacks the bird *being chased* rather than the chaser. If the bird chased is a female, this may increase his chances of copulating with her, but it also means that several males can, in effect, cooperate to chase off an intruding or commuting bird. This may have the net effect of limiting the number or distribution of *anna* territories in some areas.

In this connection, it is noteworthy that Pitelka (1951) and Williamson (1956) emphasize that neighboring males are continually aware of one another, and periodically test and challenge one another's defenses. I agree, and would further suggest that such males can and do recognize each other *as individuals*. Should one resident be removed, others will quickly notice it and intensify their attacks on his successor, as occurred with male 16 at Franklin Canyon. After the new male is established and "familiar", the attacks of his neighbors drop off. Male 16, after his accident (see above), could perhaps have been easily routed had males 3 and 11 (fig. 10) subjected him to the same amount and intensity of attacks as they did earlier.

Each individual male *anna* on breeding territory had a relatively small number (usually between 5 and 10) of regular perches in his core area, and was extremely consistent and predictable in their use. Through the observation of marked birds, I found that these patterns of perch utilization remained fairly stable as long as the given individual controlled a particular territory. Different individuals successively holding the same territory, as in the instances of replacement cited above, had recognizably different perching patterns—although some of the same bushes might be used, seldom did two individuals use the same twigs, and almost never the same places on the twigs!

If it is indeed possible to recognize a given individual by the perches he uses, this presents an opportunity to get information on the number of successive years a given male may occupy a given territory. That is, if a male *anna* on a

---

Fig. 11. Occupation of breeding territories by *C. anna* males during the 1968-69 breeding season, along the ridgetop trail at Franklin Canyon.
  Numbers refer to individual males; males on the same horizontal line occupied the same territory successively. Male 21 occupied parts of the territories of males 1 and 3. Heavy line = full breeding territoriality. Light line = reduced defense or advertisement. Broken line = defense absent.

territory uses a particular set of perches, and if the bird occupying the territory the next year uses exactly the same perches, in the same pattern, then it could well be the same bird. Based on this kind of evidence, I have 4 instances where the same individual may have occupied the same territory in two successive years: territory A in 1966-67 and 1967-68; C and 2 in 1967-68 and 1968-69; 11 and IX, and 3 and II in 1968-69 and 1969-70. The male holding III in 1969-70 had a perching pattern virtually identical to that of the occupant(s) of 1966-67 and 1967-68, but very different from that of the previous year's bird. Unfortunately, I was unable to keep individuals marked through the annual molt, and therefore lack definite proof of territorial occupancy by the same bird in different years.

In the Santa Monica Mountains, male *anna* usually abandon their breeding territories in April and early May (see above). The abandonment of a breeding territory may not be an abrupt, all-or-none process. In some cases a male will disappear completely and suddenly from his territory. Often, however, a male's breeding territory will change more or less gradually into what is effectively a feeding territory, as he restricts his area of defense to a few food plants, sings less frequently from ever more concealed perches, chases intruders less and threatens more, etc. The male may increasingly restrict his active territorial advertisement and defense to early morning and late afternoon, becoming increasingly inactive at midday. Since these changes may take place over several days or weeks, it is difficult to pinpoint the exact time at which many individuals cease to hold breeding territories.

Many adult male *anna* apparently leave the chaparral soon after abandoning their breeding territories. Some probably go directly to the mountains at this time; of those that remain in the lowlands and foothills, most move into gardens and set up feeding territories at patches of cultivated flowers. Just prior to establishing feeding territories, some males may go through a week or so of perching low and inconspicuously, singing little, and generally avoiding aggressive activity; this phase appears to correspond to the peak of body molt.

Nesting Behavior of Female Anna Hummingbirds

There is considerable evidence that female Anna Hummingbirds spend much more time foraging for insects than do males during the breeding season (Woods, 1940; Stiles, unpublished observations). This may be partly because territorial males often control the best floral food sources, and also because females must catch a great many insects to obtain protein for egg production, and to feed to the young. However, a ready source of flower nectar is also of considerable importance to a nesting female. When incubating eggs or brooding young, female *anna* do not enter torpor at night (Howell and Dawson, 1954). They are thus deprived of an important mechanism for conserving energy (Pearson, 1954);

Lasiewski, 1963), and must be able to feed well at dawn and dusk, when suitable insects are least available. A convenient and dependable energy source is needed at these times, and this implies a floral food source.

The location of suitable flowers seems to be an important factor in a female's choice of a nest site. Before beginning to build her nest, a female will often restrict her activities to the vicinity of such a food source. She may defend it much in the manner of a male on a feeding territory, albeit usually less vigorously. She chatters aggressively and flies at intruders, but rarely chases them any distance; should an intruder refuse to leave, she may even desist. Female *anna* do not sing, but often give a burst of loud, staccato chipping while flying or perching in their feeding territories. Similar chipping is given later around the nest, and probably serves an advertising and spacing function in both cases. This is the closest approach in female *anna* to the kinds of territoriality seen in males, and supports Pitelka's (1942) contention that territoriality in female hummingbirds most closely approaches that of males in connection with food sources.

I believe that the nest site is usually chosen after the female has found a nectar source, and is located within a convenient distance of that source. Nests at Trancas Canyon were often near *Ribes* bushes. At Stone Canyon, several early nests were placed near the *Eucalyptus* grove in 1967-68 and 1969-70 when the grove was in good bloom, but not in 1968-69 when *Eucalyptus* scarcely bloomed at all. Other flowers at Stone Canyon that seemed to be important in determining the location of *anna* nests were *Strelitzia*, *Abutilon*, and *Fuchsia*. Once the nest site is chosen, the female begins to defend it as well. At this point, the "nesting territory" consists of the nest site and feeding rights at some flower clump. Also included in a female's regular rounds are one or several prominent perches from which she launches insect-catching sallies, or upon which she may spend considerable time resting or preening. A female manifests considerable intolerance of other hummingbirds at these perches, but rarely actually defends them. Should another hummer land, she may chip or even chatter but rarely attacks, and sometimes ignores the other altogether.

Once incubation has begun, the time and energy demands of reproduction increasingly preclude the defense of anything but the nest site itself. During the latter part of incubation, female *anna* may ignore other hummers foraging at the flowers she formerly defended, unless she herself is feeding there at the time. On such occasions she will chatter and fly at the intruder, but usually not chase it for any distance. Such behavior of female *anna* at food sources closely resembles that of those male *anna* that commute to food sources outside of their breeding territory. Defense of the nectar source is practically nonexistent during the period when the young are being fed; the female may range widely in quest of insects at this time.

I did not attempt to color-mark females and hence could not follow individuals through the breeding season with certainty. However, some females were nearly as regular and consistent as males in their use of certain perches. I obtained renesting data for several such females at Stone Canyon. Sites of later renestings were usually within a short distance of the earlier nest(s), especially if the original floral food supply was still present. In a typical instance, a nest with eggs was destroyed by tree pruners on 22 February 1968. The female built her second nest 8 meters from the first, and continued to feed at the *Strelitzia* patch 30 meters away. Eggs were laid in the second nest around 5 March and hatched about the twentieth, but the young had disappeared on the twenty-eighth. Another female made 4 unsuccessful nesting attempts in a 25-meter radius between 17 January and 24 March 1969. A female that successfully raised two broods laid her eggs about 1-5 February and 25-30 March; the young fledged approximately 15 March and 10 May, respectively. I know of no female that successfully raised 3 broods.

TABLE 10

COMPARATIVE NESTING SUCCESS OF NORTH AMERICAN HUMMINGBIRDS

Species	Number of nests of known or probable fate	Number of nests in which:			Percent success of		Source
		eggs were laid	young hatched	young fledged	all nests of known or probable fate	all nests in which eggs were laid	
Calypte anna							
Stone Canyon	63	51	32	23	36.6	45.2	Present
Trancas Canyon	22	17	10	7	32.0	41.5	Study
Total	85	68	42	30	31.3	44.2	
Santa Cruz	20	16	—	8	40.0	50.0	Legg & Pitelka, 1956
Calypte costae	—	29	—	12	—	41.4	Woods, 1927
Archilochus alexandri							
Stone Canyon	31	26	14	8	25.8	30.7	
Franklin Canyon	14	12	7	4	28.6	33.3	Present
Trancas Canyon	10	9	6	3	30.0	33.3	study
Total	55	47	27	15	27.3	31.9	
Selasphorus sasin	18	16	—	4	22.2	25.0	Legg & Pitelka, 1956

The nesting success I observed for the Anna Hummingbird (table 10) was comparable to that found in previous studies on this species (Legg and Pitelka, 1956) and *C. costae* (Woods, 1927), and somewhat lower than for most of the open-nesting passerines discussed by Lack (1954). Except for the heavy rains of January 1969 (see above), weather did not appear to be a major cause of nest failure, and very few losses appeared to be due to direct human interference. Predation appears to be the commonest cause of nest failure, though on only one occasion did I actually witness a nest being robbed (by a Scrub Jay, *Aphelocoma caerulescens*). I have seen female *anna* mobbing Scrub Jays, Mockingbirds (*Mimus polyglottos*), and Bullock's Orioles (*Icterus bullockii*), and on one occasion a Gopher Snake (*Pituophis catenifer*); all of these may prey to some extent on *anna* eggs and/or young. A mobbing female hovers within a meter or two of the potential predator, giving a high, rapid, excited-sounding version of the staccato chipping described above. Sometimes she may hover within a few centimeters of the predator, making rapid darts at its head and back.

Behavior of Prebreeding Spring Transients

The Rufous Hummingbird is by far the most important spring transient in terms of numbers, belligerence, and effects on the activities of Anna Hummingbirds. Allen Hummingbirds pass through the Los Angeles area in January and early February, but generally keep close to the coast. They feed largely at *Eucalyptus* groves, and are seen in chaparral areas in very small numbers, if at all. Calliope Hummingbirds are seen mostly in very late March and early April, usually in small numbers and associated with the much more numerous *rufus*. The Calliope is the smallest North American hummingbird, and is subordinate to *rufus* and *anna* (table 11).

Rufous Hummingbirds begin arriving in the Santa Monica Mountains area in early to mid-March, and all except an occasional straggler have usually left by mid-April. There is great variation in the numbers of *rufus* in the chaparral from year to year, apparently depending in part on the amount of *Eucalyptus* blooming in the Los Angeles Basin at the time. 1967 and 1969 were poor *Eucalyptus* years at Stone and Franklin Canyons and several other nearby localities, and *rufus* numbers in the chaparral reached levels far higher than at any time in 1968, which was a good year for *Eucalyptus*. Numbers of *rufus* fluctuate widely from day to day, suggesting a rapid turnover of individuals (see fig. 9). Of 5 males and 6 females marked on 31 March 1968, only one female was still present in the area a week later.

A number of *rufus* will often move en masse into a good patch of *Ribes*, sometimes taking over prime feeding areas from *anna* males. This they seem able to do because of numbers and persistence. On a one-to-one basis, an established *anna* male is nearly always able to expel any *rufus* from his territory. Individual *rufus* rarely attack male *anna*, and are even more rarely successful (table 11). However, if several *rufus* try to settle at once in his territory, a male *anna* is often unable to eject them all: while he chases one, another enters, etc. Eventually

TABLE 11

Dominance relations among Chaparral Hummingbirds, Franklin Canyon, April-May 1968 and 1969

		Aggressive encounters lost							Totals won	Percent of interspecific encounters won
		C.a. ♂♂	C.a. juv.	A.a. ♂♂	C.c. ♂♂	S.r. ♂♂	S.r. ♀♀	S.c. ♂♂		
Aggressive encounters won	C.a. ♂♂	52	68	34	23	19	12	2	210	84.4
	C.a. juv.	13	85	15	2	4	2	2	123	41.7
	A.a. ♂♂	12	31	49	15	1	0	1	109	47.3
	C.c. ♂♂	2	18	9	16	0	0	1	46	40.0
	S.r. ♂♂	2	7	5	1	19	9	6	49	46.7
	S.r. ♀♀	3	3	4	3	10	13	8	44	60.0
	S.c. ♂♂	0	1	0	0	0	0	4	5	5.0
Totals lost		84	213	116	60	53	36	24	586	

his defense becomes less vigorous, and he is forced to abandon part of his territory. Once more or less established the *rufus* defend small, often close-packed feeding territories containing 1 or 2 *Ribes* bushes each. They hold these territories for a few hours up to a week or more. If a male *anna* attempts to attack one *rufus*, he may be attacked in turn by 2 or 3 others as the fray passes through or over their territories. A single established *rufus* may sometimes hold its position against an attacking *anna* male, and may even force it to retreat, but *rufus* rarely chase *anna* for any distance.

Once the *rufus* have become established, interspecific aggression drops off markedly. Usually *rufus* perch low and inconspicuously, thus not inviting *anna* attack. They keep to their feeding territories except for periodic foraging forays to neighboring *Ribes* bushes, which often heighten the intraspecific aggression among the *rufus*. Anna males attack *rufus* less often. Presumably the cost, in time and energy, of attempting to expel several established *rufus* is prohibitive; and *rufus* rarely attack *anna* in any case.

It is of particular interest that female *rufus* hold feeding territories on an essentially equal basis with males, and are frequently more aggressive and successful in territorial defense. Cody (1968) has also found female territoriality among various *Selasphorus* in spring migration on the Mojave Desert. Dive displays by male *rufus* are rarely seen in March but become progressively more frequent in April.

Migrating *Selasphorus* frequently settle en masse in certain rich feeding areas and hardly at all at nearby sites, even if the quantitative difference in food available seems slight. This tendency to concentrate in one place is partly balanced by the presence of feeding territoriality, which produces some degree of spacing of birds within the feeding area. The value of this apparent gregariousness is probably twofold: it may attract other birds to rich food sites and result in enhanced social stimulation of feeding and coordination of migratory movements, and it may facilitate taking over feeding areas already occupied and defended by *anna* males.

No individuals of *calliope* hold feeding territories consistently, although males may display. This may reflect the Calliope's subordinate status: it is usually only able to utilize the poorer or more scattered food sources, or must try to poach from the territories of more dominant hummers at richer food sources. For example, on 8 April 1969 at Stone Canyon, I found a small *Pittosporum* tree in flower, which at 0700 had been divided up into feeding territories by 3 *rufus*: 1 male, 2 females. Territorial defense was vigorous, and the 3 or 4 *calliope* males trying to feed there had little success. By 0900 the *rufus* were present only occasionally, and by 1000 the *calliope* had the tree to themselves. Two males used about half the tree each, with very little aggression. The decrease in *rufus* activity reflected the progressive exhaustion of the tree's nectar supply, which by 1000 was so low that presumably only the little *calliope* could efficiently forage there. By 1030 no hummingbirds were using the tree at all, and I was unable to obtain appreciable nectar from the flowers at this time. At other *Pittosporum* trees in the area, early-morning nectar collections yielded an average of 5 to 8 microliters of nectar per flower.

The activities of Rufous Hummingbirds may interfere seriously with breeding territoriality of *anna* males. By restricting access to feeding areas, groups of *rufus* may force a male *anna* to feed elsewhere, or to utilize and defend only a part of his territory. Sometimes a male *anna* will be forced to temporarily abandon his territory altogether. After a large wave of *rufus* have left, there is often a conspicuous resurgence of territorial behavior among *anna* males. Cody (1968) notes that territorial male *costae* may be similarly affected by migrating *Selasphorus* on the Mojave Desert. By contrast, *rufus* affect the nesting of *anna* females very little. They rarely penetrate the shady oak woodlands or gardens where *anna* nest in greatest numbers, and *anna* females can eject *rufus* from the vicinity of their nests. At Stone Canyon with its extensive gardens, large numbers of *rufus* congregated only at *Eucalyptus* trees.

BEHAVIOR OF BREEDING COSTA AND BLACK-CHINNED HUMMINGBIRDS

In 1968 and 1969, Costa and Black-chinned Hummingbirds arrived in the Santa Monica Mountains in early March and early April respectively and both reached their maximum abundance in late April (table 3). *Calypte costae* shows a strong preference for the drier and more open areas in and around the mountains, including southern and western exposures, the sage-covered slopes near the sea, and the oak savanna and sage on the north side of the mountains. This species is associated with the coastal sage elements of chaparral vegetation, and especially with the various shrubby species of *Salvia*, which are its preferred food source from late April through June. The rarest breeding hummingbird in the higher and wetter parts of the mountains, *costae* is the only species common in the dry chaparral and oak savanna to the north. Its major food plants in this area are *Salvia leucophylla* and *apiana*, and *Trichostema lanatum*.

Breeding territories of *costae* males are large, often 2 to 4 acres in size. There is no clearly defined core area and buffer zone as in *anna* breeding territories. The vegetation is generally low and fairly uniform in height, with higher perches, typically yucca stalks, scattered through the territory. Food, in the form of *Salvia* or less often *Diplacus* flowers, is usually widely or even continuously distributed over the territory, or in large patches. Over its whole range *costae* is probably most abundant in desert areas; its most important food plants are *Beloperone californica* and *Isomeris arborea* in the Colorado and Mojave Deserts, respectively. The distribution of these food plants bears a similar relation to the location and extent of *costae* breeding territories as does *Salvia* in the chaparral; the size and general form of the territories are similar.

Female *costae* are the only hummingbirds to build nests in the chaparral itself, frequently in or near the breeding territory of a male when this contains good feeding areas. The male does not help with nesting chores, and often chases or displays at the female when she appears. The favorite nest sites of *costae* are at some kind of break in the chaparral, either along an edge or in bushes taller than the surrounding vegetation, such that the female has a clear view of the immediate vicinity from the nest. The three *costae* nests I found in the course of the present study were in large *Rhus laurina* or *Ceanothus* bushes, in chaparral within 50 feet of the bottom of Trancas Canyon. I was shown a fourth nest by F. McCammon in a small *Rhamnus* shrub some 2 meters from a large stand of *Salvia leucophylla* in the hilly oak savanna region north of the mountains. The *Salvia*, and presumably the nest also, were within the boundaries of the breeding territory of a *costae* male. Estimated egg dates for these four *costae* nests range from 10-15 April to 25-30 May. Bent (1940) and Pitelka (1951) list egg dates from chaparral areas between mid-March and late June, the peak of the nesting season being May and early June.

The relative scarcity of *costae* in the chaparral before late April is interesting, since I have found them breeding in the Borrego Desert of Southern California as early as mid-February. In early March 1969 I found nests of *costae* in all stages in this region, and by late March fledged young were seen. By late April, *costae* had practically disappeared from the Borrego Desert, except for a few juveniles; their major food plant, *Beloperone*, had all but ceased blooming. It seems not unlikely that many *costae* may raise one brood in the desert in early spring, then move into the chaparral in mid- to late April and breed again. The species does not appear in numbers in the higher mountains between the desert and the chaparral during late spring (Grinnell, 1908; Grinnell and Swarth, 1913; R. Adams, personal communication), and certainly its stay in the Colorado Desert is insufficient to permit the raising of more than one brood there (cf. Woods, 1927).

Costa Hummingbirds may winter in small numbers in the Santa Monica Mountains in some years. Between November 1969 and February 1970, I saw at least one adult and one first-year male *costae* in the Franklin Canyon chaparral, and one first-year male at Stone Canyon. These individuals were invariably subordinate to the *anna* males of the area, and were routed when they tried to feed at *Ribes* in or near *anna* territories. Song and display dives were given by adult male *costae*, but at no time during the fall and winter could I find a *costae* male localized on a breeding territory.

Of the three breeding species, *alexandri* tends to prefer the most mesic sites. Male *alexandri* establish breeding territories on lower north- or east-facing canyon slopes in tall, broken chaparral mixed with oaks, or in canyon-bottom clearings. The most important feature of the male's territory seems to be the physiognomy of the vegetation—an open, flat to gently sloping area ca. 15-30 meter in diameter, flanked on (usually) at least two sides by much taller vegetation, in or on which the bird perches. The territory differs from that of *anna* in that the surrounding vegetation averages taller, often shutting off the view of what, in *anna*, would be the buffer zone; in fact, the whole *alexandri* territory is roughly the size of the *anna* core area. Good feeding areas, usually *Diplacus*, are always nearby, although not necessarily in the territory itself. In some areas, tall stands of *Nicotiana* may serve both as food supply and the requisite higher vegetation.

Female *alexandri* nest in canyon-bottom woodlands in the same areas as *anna*, but show a much stronger tendency to place their nests over water, hence, nests are placed in sycamores more often than oaks. Here too, physiognomy of the vegetation is important: in the absence of a convenient stream, the nest will be placed in vegetation overhanging any suitably flat, bare area, such as a road, walk, path, or garden clearing. The nest site averages considerably lower than that of *anna*. The nesting season extends from late April through July, but there is a single large peak of egg laying from mid-May to early June (see also Pitelka, 1951). Since approximately 6 weeks are required for a single complete nesting cycle, it seems doubtful that many females will raise more than one brood per year in the Santa Monica Mountains. There seems to be no evidence that a second brood is raised at higher elevations, as Bene (1946) suggested for *alexandri* in Arizona.

Nesting success of *alexandri* was lower than that of *anna* (table 10). The lower nest sites may have resulted in greater human interference, but I also suspect that predation was greater on *alexandri* nests. Each of the first 6 nests I found at Stone Canyon in 1968 was robbed shortly after egg laying; on one occasion I observed the eggs being taken by a female Bullock's Oriole, *Icterus bullockii*. I frequently saw female *alexandri* mobbing female orioles in early May, and suspect that these were important predators on *alexandri* nests. On another occasion in lower Franklin Canyon, I found a Gopher Snake (*Pituophis catenifer*) crawling along a low horizontal branch of deodar cedar, at the tip of which was an empty *alexandri* nest.

Female *alexandri* have a well-known habit of using the golden-yellow down of sycamore leaves in nest construction (Dawson, 1923; Bent, 1940). When the nests are placed in sycamore trees, as is usually the case in the wild, they are thereby exceedingly well camouflaged. However, when nests built of sycamore down are placed in vegetation of a different color, as often happens in gardens, they may be quite conspicuous. This probably accounts for the higher nesting success of *alexandri* in Trancas Canyon (table 10). In Franklin Canyon in 1970, 2 of 4 *alexandri* nests in sycamores were successful, but only 1 of 7 in the dark-needled deodar cedars.

Nesting of *alexandri* may vary greatly from year to year in a single locality, and this appears to correlate with the amount of rain in the preceding winter. In the relatively wet years of 1968 and 1969 I found 4 and 6 *alexandri* nests respectively in Trancas Canyon. In these years Trancas Creek flowed all summer, but in 1970 the creek was dry from February on. Intensive searches in April, May, and June 1970 disclosed no sign of nesting by *alexandri*; in fact, this species was not seen at all in Trancas Canyon after early May. By contrast, in the well-watered gardens at Stone Canyon, I found 10 *alexandri* nests in 1970, compared with 8, 11, and 14 in the three previous years. Also in 1970, I found 16 *alexandri* nests in and around similarly well-watered gardens at Franklin Canyon.

As *costae* and *alexandri* are reaching peak abundances, the *anna* breeding season is drawing to a close. *C. costae* shows relatively slight habitat overlap with *anna*, and is probably too thinly distributed to affect *anna* much in any case. On the other hand, *alexandri* overlaps rather broadly with *anna* in several habitat parameters. The two species often nest in close proximity, and in both 1968 and 1969 one or two chaparral sites were occupied in sequence by *anna* and *alexandri* males. However, until they begin to molt heavily, *anna* males are usually dominant to males of *alexandri* or *costae* (table 11) such that appearance of these species does not, in itself, disrupt territorial or feeding behavior of *anna*.

In the oak woodlands and gardens, I saw very little interspecific aggression between *alexandri* and *anna* females, either at flowers or nesting sites, even though both species were often present together in fairly high numbers, and nested in the same areas. The two species tended to use different flowers to some extent: at Stone Canyon, *alexandri* favored *Abutilon*, *Heuchera*, *Jacobinia*, and *Hamelia*, as well as *Nicotiana* and *Diplacus* at the edge of the adjacent chaparral, while *anna* visited *Abutilon*, *Fuchsia*, *Cuphea*, *Cestrum*, and *Strelitzia*. Most of the interspecific aggression at flowers took place at a large *Abutilon* bush in the garden grove, which was visited frequently by both species. When feeding rights were disputed *anna* females were sufficiently dominant that *alexandri* females usually gave way without a fight. Nest sites were plentiful, and most agression related to nesting appeared to be intraspecific. I have no data to suggest that *anna* excludes *alexandri* from potential nesting areas or vice versa comparable to those of Legg and Pitelka (1956) for *anna* and *Selasphorus sasin*.

Bene (1946) states that aggressive behavior in female *alexandri* defending feeders reaches a peak during nest site selection and building, and declines thereafter—exactly comparable to the situation in *anna*. In my experience, *alexandri* females are often much less vigorous and consistent than *anna* in defending food sources, perhaps because of the presence of the more dominant *anna*, or because flowers in general are much more abundant and widely distributed by the time *alexandri* begins to nest.

Behavior of Juvenile Anna Hummingbirds

After fledging, young Anna Hummingbirds remain more or less dependent upon the female for perhaps one to two weeks. This is the phase of the life history of *anna* with which I am least familiar, for I have never succeeded in following a fledgling through to independence. For the first day or two the fledgling may remain in the vicinity of the nest, possibly returning to it at night. Fledglings I have observed at this stage perched for long periods, usually in thick vegetation, frequently buzzing their wings and occasionally making flights of a few centimeters to several meters. They orient quickly toward any small moving objects such as flying insects, and probe at various kinds of small, dark specks on their perches or on nearby leaves. At this stage, the young birds are entirely dependent upon the female for food, and are fed by her several times an hour. When any hummingbird passes by, they gape at it, and may give a high, piercing "seet" note. This note is also given without any obvious external stimuli if the female has not fed the young bird for some time.

At a slightly later stage, I have seen young *anna* hovering about in vegetation and darting after flying insects, often with notably less agility than adults. They may still beg from passing hummingbirds but are much less frequently fed by the female, and appear capable of feeding for themselves for the most part. I have not seen young *anna* at this stage forage at flowers, and do not know at what point they begin to feed on nectar.

When first seen in the chaparral, most juvenile *anna* are usually fully independent and feeding for themselves, upon nectar as well as insects. At this stage, they effectively constitute a separate ecological entity from adult *anna*. The young birds move into good *Ribes* areas that are either undefended, or in such tall and broken chaparral that a territorial male *anna* cannot easily eject them. Like migrant *rufus*, groups of young *anna* can sometimes take over a feeding area from an adult male *anna* by virtue of numbers and persistence. Frequently local concentrations of juveniles appear where the feeding area is both rich and difficult for an adult male to defend. As groups of *rufus* vacate the areas they have taken over from *anna* males, numbers of young *anna* may move in.

Juvenile Anna Hummingbirds show rudimentary territorial behavior at an extremely early age. I have seen birds whose bills were as yet but 3/4 of full length (and who therefore could not have been long out of the nest) defending *Ribes* bushes, and even attempting to expel adult males. Some young males were attempting to sing and give display dives at this early age, before even the first red feathers had appeared on the throat or crown. Precocious aggressive and/or display activity, with a greater or lesser degree of territorial site attachment, has also been described for *anna* by Pitelka (1951), Legg and Pitelka (1956), and Ortiz (1967).

The territorial activities of young *anna* affect adult males on breeding territories in much the same way as do migrating *rufus*. That is, they invade feeding areas in numbers, such that the expenditures of time and energy required to expel them may be prohibitive for an adult male. By moving onto a male's feeding preserve, the young increase the energy he requires to defend it, while at the same time depriving him of some or all of his territory's energy resources. This erodes the male's effectiveness in territorial defense until he is forced to abandon part or all of his territory. According to Ortiz (1967), juvenile *sasin* may have the same effect on adult males of that species.

Young *anna* often appear in the chaparral in two's, perhaps nest mates (see also Ortiz, 1967). Among the younger juveniles, most aggressive interactions take place between the members of sibling (?) pairs, who will chase or display at one another by the hour. One bird will fly over to another's *Ribes* bush and feed, or dive at the owner, or try to bump him off his perch; the second will attack or give chase, and may then fly over to challenge the first—and so on for much of the day, with periodic recesses for resting, feeding, and preening. The general impression I get from watching these young birds is that they are engaged in play, quite comparable to that described in many young mammals.

Although there is considerable subjective agreement among many authors as to what constitutes play behavior, it is very difficult to arrive at an objective definition (Mason 1965; Marler and Hamilton 1966). However, many of the commonly cited elements of play are present in groups of *anna* juveniles: the peer-group, presence of components of adult behavior patterns in incomplete or temporally reorganized sequences, the suggestion of "practice" of social behaviors that will later be important in territoriality and mating. The performance of these maneuvers appears to be its own reward, and aggressive interactions never conclude with the actual fighting somtimes seen in adult males, in which the combatants fall to earth locked together by bills or feet, and attempt to beat each other with their wings.

There has been much ink spilled in the literature on the question of whether the high degree of aggressive and territorial activity of hummingbirds in general is a manifestation of playfulness, "excessive exuberance," or some such quality. The whole question has been so befogged by anthropomorphism that it is difficult to conclude much from most existing accounts. I would submit that true play does occur in these groups of young birds, whereas it seldom does in adults. Adult aggressive and sexual behavior is directly concerned with survival and reproductive success, and the high degree of belligerence seen in most hummingbirds is explicable in terms of the resources for which they compete (see below). A cautionary note is sounded by Loizos (1966), who states that no clear distinction between "playful" and "serious" activity of young animals yet exists, and that while playing, young animals may equally well be performing various acts at the maximum of efficiency for their stage of development.

The amorphous, gurgling song and irregular, incomplete dives of the young juvenile male gradually approach the highly structured, ritualized performance of the adult male over a period of several months. Members of sibling (?) pairs associate less and less, and the juveniles gradually become less gregarious, less "playful". Ortiz (1967) mentions that "aggressivity" in young *anna* is present from the first, but that site attachment (and hence, territoriality) develops more slowly. In my experience, some young *anna* show site attachment from the first; others develop it gradually, still others not at all. In most cases, those showing the highest degree of territoriality are males (but it is not always possible to sex young birds in the field). Of 4 juvenile *anna* marked at a feeding area on 31 March 1968, one was seen occasionally in the same area and at two other nearby sites, and two (both males) remained territorial in the area until 12 April and 10 May (by which time the *Ribes* had ceased to bloom).

Ortiz (1967) reports instances of young male *anna* holding the same territory through the summer and fall in the Berkeley Botanical Garden. I have no fully comparable records of this, as most *anna* in Southern California leave the lowlands for the high mountains during the summer months. The few individuals remaining in gardens were usually adult males, who controlled most of the good food sources. I was unable to follow a single young male through the entire summer at a single site. In the fall, however, first-year *anna* males frequently hold territories at *Nicotiana* and *Eucalyptus*, along with adult males.

Precocious aggressive behavior comparable to that seen in *anna* occurs in many and perhaps all other North American hummingbirds. I have observed such behavior in *costae* and *alexandri*, and Ortiz (1967) has good descriptions of juvenile territoriality in *sasin* and *rufus*. Bene (1946) describes defense of feeding stations by young *alexandri*. The selective value of this behavior, aside from its possible importance as "practice", is that it may enable juveniles to gain access to feeding areas, particularly those that are already occupied by adult males of *anna* or other species. For instance, in one area at Franklin Canyon in which young *anna* held territories at *Ribes*, they defeated *alexandri* males in 9 of 14 aggressive encounters in early May of 1968; elsewhere, *alexandri* males won 23 of 27 encounters ($x^2 = 13.1$; $p < 0.01$). The first few weeks following fledging and/or independence are critical in the life of any small bird, and precocious territoriality, along with a tendency to aggregate, may be important in enabling young hummingbirds to survive this crucial period.

Behavior of Postbreeding Summer Residents

Postbreeding Allen Hummingbirds, *S. sasin*, arrive in numbers in the Santa Monica Mountains area in late May or June (table 3). At first there is a high proportion of adult males, but by late June and July most birds seen are juveniles. By late July and August adult and juvenile Rufous Hummingbirds, *S. rufus*, are also becoming common. Juvenile *rufus* and *sasin* are indistinguishable in the field, and can be identified with certainty in the hand only by measurements (Stiles, 1971b and 1972). However, in July most birds I caught and measured were *sasin*; in September, most were *rufus*, suggesting that the latter gradually replace the former in the study area over the summer.

Between mid-March and early May 1969, I saw occasional adult male *sasin* at Franklin Canyon. One male was seen holding a feeding territory along with a group of migrant *rufus* from 11 to 24 March. In April, a *sasin* male took over a *Nicotiana* feeding area from an *anna* male, causing the latter to leave the area, and remained vigorously territorial, giving full display dives, until his disappearance in early May. Another *sasin* male excluded two *alexandri* males from a *Diplacus* feeding site in the canyon bottom in late April, but was gone by May. Whether these birds were postbreeding or merely strays is problematical, but their overall effect on breeding hummingbirds was slight.

Those *sasin* arriving in late May and June were definitely postbreeding, and nearly always settled in *Nicotiana* stands. At first, large territories were set up and display dives and long chases were frequent, especially by adult males. By July, however, most *Selasphorus* (by this time probably both *rufus* and *sasin* were present) were occupying small, often close-packed feeding territories. *Selasphorus* were usually dominant to *alexandri* and *costae* at *Nicotiana*, and could also expel those *anna* juveniles they encountered. Contact between *Selasphorus* and *anna* was relatively slight until the latter began to return from their summer stay in the high mountains in September and early October. During most of the summer, the few *anna* left in the lowlands remained in shaded gardens, where *Selasphorus* were rarely seen.

During September and early October, both *anna* and *Selasphorus* occupied *Nicotiana* stands in large numbers (cf. table 4). *Selasphorus* feeding territories tended to be smaller and much more close-packed; several *Selasphorus* often occupied the central portions of large *Nicotiana* clumps. The feeding territories of *anna* were larger, and usually encompassed smaller or scattered clumps of *Nicotiana* or were located on the peripheries of large ones. Most aggressive behavior was intraspecific, and chases and supplantings were especially frequent in the much more crowded *Selasphorus* zone. In individual conflicts, *anna* were victorious more often than not, but they were unable to penetrate areas held by *Selasphorus* because they were usually attacked by several birds in turn. This collective superiority of *Selasphorus* enabled them to control the richest feeding areas. Ortiz (1967) also notes the strong tendency of juvenile *Selasphorus* to form aggregations of small, close-packed territories. Whereas *anna* juveniles often first appear in two's Ortiz asserts that *sasin* juveniles frequently come in three's or four's, and are more gregarious from the first. He states that 5 *sasin* juveniles can coexist in the same amount of space held by a single adult male *sasin* or *anna*. As *Selasphorus* began leaving my study areas in early October 1968, I had an opportunity to obtain data on this point. At Malibu Creek, several large stands (and a number of small, scattered plants) of *Nicotiana* supported feeding territories of 6 *anna* males (including 4 adults) and 23 *Selasphorus* juveniles on 27 September. The largest number of territorial *anna* males to fit into this same area thereafter was 15 (8 adult, 7 first-year) on 19 October (table 5). However, as the *Nicotiana* was declining in flowering at this time, these figures may not be fully comparable.

ANALYSIS

This section summarizes and interprets the spatial and temporal relationships between food supply, climate, competition, and events of the annual cycle in the Anna Hummingbird. The food of greatest relevance here is nectar, which is crucial in breeding territoriality and nesting. Food supply is considered as both a proximate and ultimate factor in its effects on breeding and seasonal movements. The evolution of the territorial and mating system of the Anna Hummingbird is discussed in terms of dispersion of floral food resources.

Food Supply and the Annual Cycle in Time and Space
The initiation of breeding: proximate factors

In birds, it is usually the male who comes into breeding condition first, and appropriate psychic stimulation from the male is necessary to bring the female into full reproductive condition (see reviews by Lehrman, 1964; Lack, 1966). Several possible advantages for early testicular maturation by males of territorial species have been discussed by Orians (1961). These include early occupation of territories, the psychological advantage of prior residence in territorial fights, and the opportunity to mate with the first females to come into breeding condition. Especially in a promiscuous species like the Anna Hummingbird, this may result in the fertilization of more females over the course of the breeding season. As discussed earlier, the first Anna males into an area take over the best feeding areas, which may also result in enhanced mating success (see below).

For the female, on the other hand, early achievement of breeding condition may not, in itself, be an advantage (Orians, 1961). The maturation of ovaries and egg production are so much more expensive than testicular maturation and sperm production, that the appearance of optimal environmental conditions is much more important for the female. The initiation of laying in females is often dependent upon the appearance of appropriate temperatures or food resources (reviews by Lack, 1966; Lofts and Murton, 1968). Thus, one would expect the female to lag behind the male in attaining breeding condition. In *Calypte anna*, the females' nesting season lags several weeks behind the initiation of male breeding territoriality (cf. table 3). Thus, in discussing the ecological factors regulating timing and duration of breeding in the Anna Hummingbird, attention naturally focuses upon those factors that affect male breeding territoriality.

The initiation of breeding territoriality in the Anna Hummingbird was studied by Williamson (1956), with reference to the relation between behavior and events of the molt and testis cycles. He defined 5 histologic stages of the recrudescing

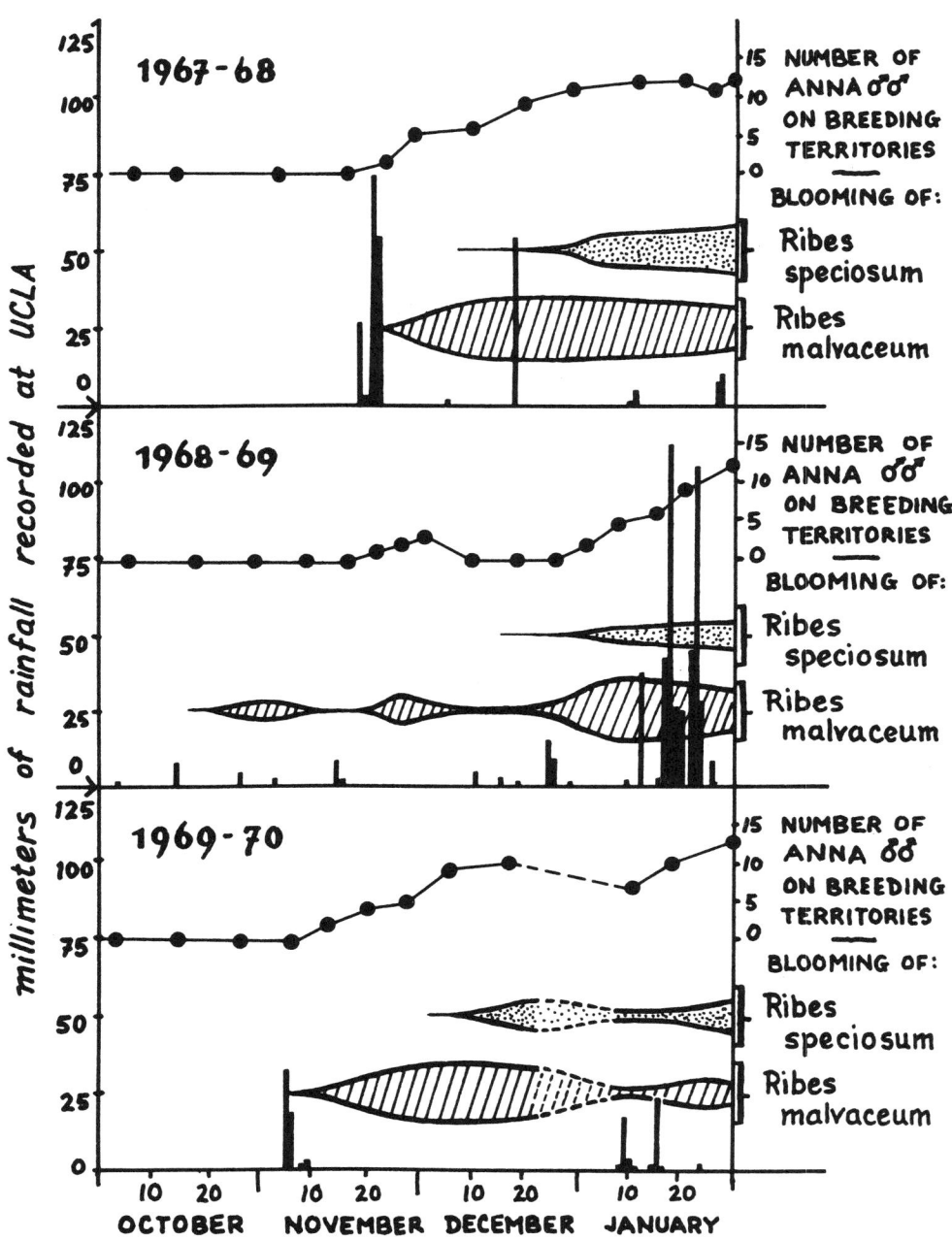

Fig. 12. Rainfall patterns, blooming of *Ribes malvaceum* and *speciosum*, and initiation of breeding territoriality by *C. anna* males along the ridgetop trail at Franklin Canyon during three different years.

testis, with full breeding condition corresponding to stage 5. He found that all males in stages 4 and 5, and a few in earlier stages, finished the annual molt and suggested that completion of molt was necessary for attainment of breeding condition. He also found that all birds collected on breeding territories were in stage 5. After the onset of the heavy winter rains in December, all birds collected had mature sperm in the testes. A serious weakness of Williamson's data is that he collected only 2 birds during the crucial period of 21 November-21 December. Also, he does not include any consideration of food supply in his analysis.

Testis volumes, molt stage, and territorial status of male *anna* I collected between October 1968 and January 1969 are presented in figure 8. Unfortunately, histologic analysis of testes was not possible, but an examination of Williamson's data indicates that no individual with a testis volume of 1 mm^3 was in less than stage 4, and that all individuals with a testis volume of over 3 mm^3 had attained stage 5. Rainfall, blooming of *Ribes*, and attainment of breeding territoriality by male *anna* in three different years of the present study are discussed at length above, and summarized graphically in figure 12 (see also table 3).

Several conclusions emerge from a survey of these data. First, in male *anna* testicular maturation and attainment of breeding territoriality follow closely the onset of heavy winter rains, as was also found by Williamson (1956). Blooming of *Ribes malvaceum* is also closely correlated with the start of the rains. Second, the locus of territorial behavior is strongly correlated with the blooming of suitable food plants: male *anna* do not move into chaparral areas to set up breeding territories unless *Ribes* is blooming there, or *Eucalyptus* is available nearby. Third, some birds not quite through the annual molt in November 1968 had very enlarged testes and were holding breeding territories. However, molt in these specimens was restricted to a few tardy crown and gorget feathers in each case; this does not greatly undermine the general validity of Williamson's (1956) conclusions. Fourth, hot and dry weather following the rains exerts a depressing effect on both *Ribes* blooming and territorial activity, but males remain in the chaparral as long as the *Ribes* lasts. And finally, full breeding territoriality will not appear much earlier than mid-November, even if rain falls and *Ribes* blooms.

The last of these conclusions deserves further consideration. In October 1968, a combination of rainfall and *Ribes* was not followed by breeding territoriality, while a similar combination in late November was. Although *anna* males were moving into the chaparral by 10-15 November 1969, and a few display dives were seen, many males still exhibited some of the signs of feeding, rather than breeding territoriality—song from low perches (sometimes actually in the *Ribes* plant itself), chipping instead of singing when an observer walked by, etc. It was not until 20-25 November that all males were showing full breeding territoriality. It is noteworthy that full breeding territoriality appeared at nearly the same time in all three years: 22-24 November 1967, 18-25 November 1968, and 15-25 November 1969. This strongly suggests the existence of some underlying physiological cycle that regulates the period during which the male *anna* can attain full breeding condition, perhaps through stimulation by rainfall or associated temperature changes. The fact that nearly all male *anna* completed the annual molt by about the same time also suggests such a conclusion, in accordance with the widely held belief that the hormonal bases of molt and breeding are to some degree antagonistic. Such a similarity in the timing of reproductive events in different years by a temperate-zone bird almost invariably implies the existence of a photoperiodic mechanism. This inference is supported by Williamson's (1956) discovery that some male *anna* attained stage 4 of testes development as early as mid-October, but no birds in stage 5 were found until December. However, I strongly emphasize that field studies such as mine and Williamson's can only establish *correlations* between environmental and physiological events, and that controlled laboratory experiments are necessary to establish *causality*.

Experimentation to prove the existence of a photoperiodically controlled sensitive period in the Anna Hummingbird would be exceedingly interesting on a number of counts. To my knowledge, no photoresponsive temperate-zone bird yet studied regularly begins to breed during short and decreasing daylengths. To be sure, short daylengths are required by many species to terminate postbreeding refractoriness, and under certain environmental conditions, many such birds can be stimulated to sexual activity or even breeding in late fall and winter (see review by Lofts and Murton, 1968). Williamson (1956) notes that in *anna* the testes are recrudescing during the hottest time of year, and temperature appears to be the most important modifier of the gonad cycle at this stage in many species (Lofts and Murton, 1968). In these respects, the Anna Hummingbird resembles fairly closely a large number of temperate-zone birds whose gonads respond to daylength in anticipating the season appropriate for breeding. The major difference seems to lie in the kind of environmental accelerators (in the sense of Marshall, 1961) to which the Anna Hummingbird responds, and perhaps in the threshold of this response. In the rapidity with which rainfall and the appearance of appropriate food are followed by breeding activity, the Anna Hummingbird brings to mind the Red-billed Dioch, *Quelea* (Marshall and Disney, 1957).

Some further consideration of the initiation of nesting of female *anna* seems warranted at this point, even though data on many important points are scarce or lacking. My data (cf. table 3) do not permit inferences regarding possible photoperiodic mechanisms, or the relative importance of psychic stimulation by male *anna* and food supply. However, it is worth noting that *Ribes malvaceum* always blooms 1 to 3 weeks later in the canyon bottoms than on chapparal slopes, probably reflecting the cooler and shadier microclimate of the former (see above). Therefore, in the wild, flowers suitable for nesting females become available later than for males. In gardens, suitable flowers may bloom all fall (cf. fig. 4), but be unavailable because controlled by male *anna*. At Stone Canyon in November-December 1968, nesting activity among *anna* females was not seen in the main oak grove until after the *anna* males ceased to hold feeding territories at the *Abutilon* and *Fuchsia* there.

In the light of present information, a number of old reports and statements regarding the breeding season of the Anna Hummingbird can now be reevaluated. Bowles (1910) reported seeing a female feeding a recently fledged young on 3 January 1910, which means that the eggs would probably have been laid around 25 November of 1909. Although Pitelka (1951) considers this report improbable, I am inclined to think it reliable: my evidence on testis volumes (fig. 8) indicates that at least some males of the population would be capable of fertilizing a female by that date, and since most males can attain full territorial behavior at about this time, the requisite psychic stimulation would also be present. I seriously doubt that breeding could take place any earlier than this, however. The statements of some early authors that *anna* "breeds every month of the year" (Dawson, 1923) seem highly doubtful and are to my knowledge not substantiated by nests, eggs, or other data.

PROXIMATE FACTORS INFLUENCING TERMINATION OF BREEDING

There has been surprisingly little work done on the proximate factors that influence cessation of breeding in birds. Comparative ecological information is scarce, beyond the well-known fact that in most temperate-zone species, breeding ceases while day lengths are still stimulating and food is still abundant (Lofts and Murton, 1968). Superficially at least, this appears to be true of the Anna Hummingbird: males abandon their breeding territories and females cease egg laying before the summer solstice, and at a time when the chaparral food supply is at or near its annual maximum (fig. 3, 5, 7).

In this section I shall focus on those factors that influence the breakdown of breeding territoriality of male *anna* in April and May. Female *anna* will apparently try to continue nesting as late as they can, perhaps until food or some other environmental resource becomes limiting. The latest recorded clutches of eggs in 1968 and 1969 were completed around 5 and 22 May, respectively. These dates are within a week of the latest dates I found *anna* males on breeding territories in each year (see table 3). Nest-building occurred later in May in both years, but no more eggs were laid. These data suggest that the length of the *anna* nesting season may be limited, at least in part, by the availability of males capable of fertilizing females.

A number of factors may play a role in the decline of breeding territoriality in male *anna*. By analogy with the situation at the start of breeding, one might suspect a photoperiod-sensitive endogenous cycle, perhaps interacting with the start of the molt. Unfortunately, data on this point are limited and inconclusive. However, the relative importance of such ecological factors as weather, food supply, and competition can be profitably considered. In this connection, food

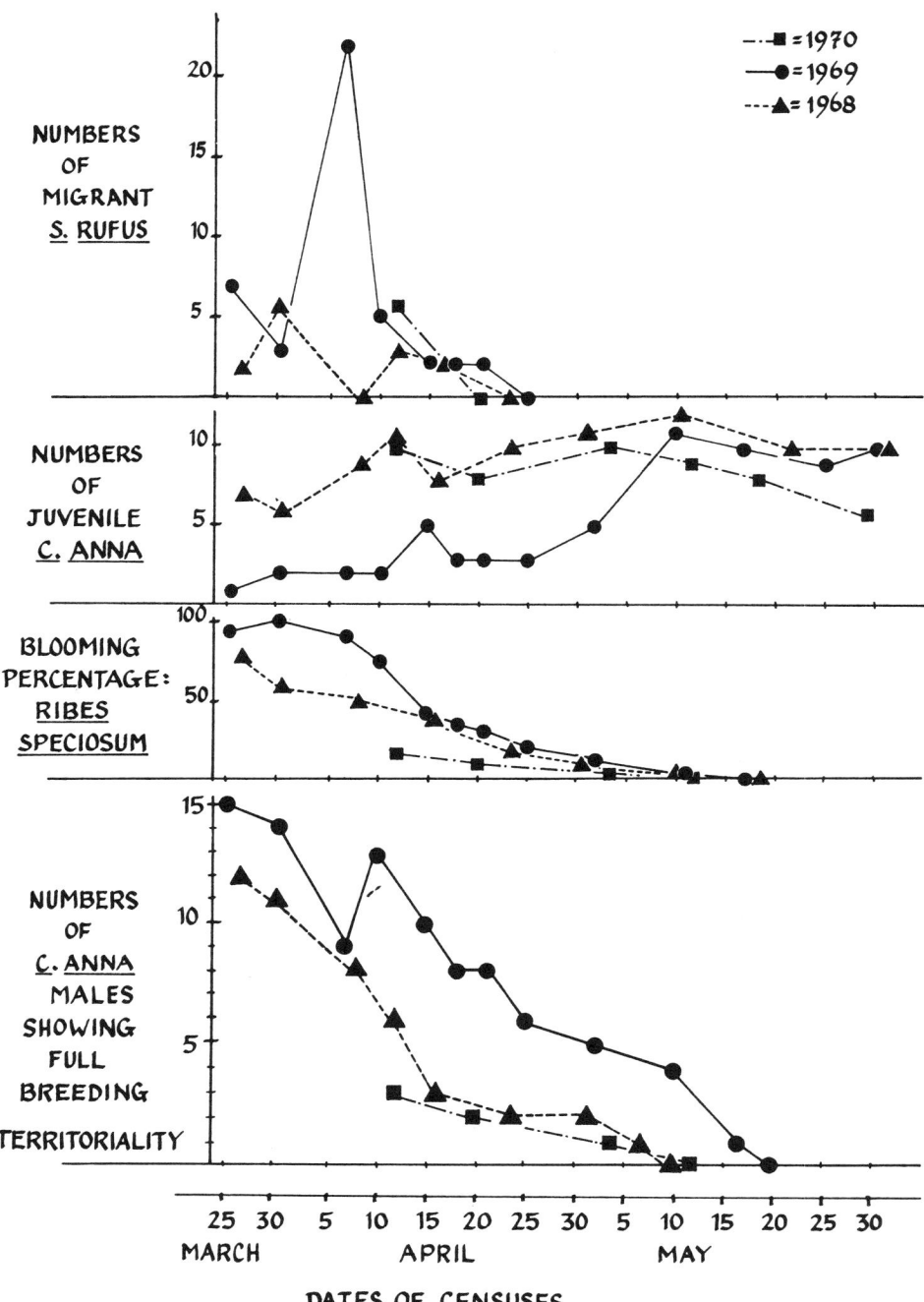

Fig. 13. Decline in breeding territoriality among *C. anna* males along the ridgetop trail at Franklin Canyon during three different years, in relation to *Ribes* supply and competition.

supply consists essentially of *Ribes* and non-*Ribes* flowers. Possible sources of increased competition include migrant *rufus*, breeding *costae* and *alexandri*, and juvenile *anna* (see above). Each of these factors will be considered in the light of comparative observations on the decline of breeding territoriality in 1968 and 1969, plus limited data from 1970. These data are summarized graphically in figure 13.

As discussed above, it is often difficult to decide at exactly what point a male *anna* ceases to hold a breeding territory. However, even allowing for this source of error, there is no doubt that breeding territoriality in male *anna* lasted longer in 1969 than in 1968. That is, more males showed more signs of breeding territoriality until later in the year in 1969, although the major decline in number of territorial males took place in mid-April in both years (fig. 13). In 1970, most male *anna* had already ceased to hold breeding territories when observations were begun on 12 April.

During the winter of 1969-70, it was seen that hot, dry weather exerted a depressing effect on breeding territoriality in male *anna*. Since the general trend of the weather in April and May is toward increasingly hot and dry conditions, one might expect this to play some role in the breakdown of breeding territoriality. Most of April 1968, however, was relatively cool. There was considerable rain early in the month, and only in the last week or so did it become really hot. Thus, at the time when most males left their territories, weather was ostensibly favorable. In 1969, most of April was very warm and dry, but late April and much of May were relatively cool and foggy. Thus, there exists no simple, direct correlation between hot weather and abandonment of breeding territories by *anna* males.

The first detectable sign of the onset of molt in male *anna* in 1968 was the loss of markings by 3 color-marked birds, all within the first 10 days of April. This was followed in each case by the abandonment of the breeding territory within 1 to 2 weeks. However, really heavy molt tends to follow, not precede, the cessation of breeding territoriality in most birds. The first signs of molt, a patchy appearance of the green dorsal feathers, were observed in mid-April in 1969 and 1970. I did not see many birds in heavy molt until well into May in 1968, and toward the end of May in 1969. In 1969, I had several cases in which an individual that was molting fairly heavily was also vigorously territorial. Thus, molt per se probably does not play a causative role in the breakdown of breeding territoriality, though it doubtless reflects the general physiological state of the bird at the time.

In both 1968 and 1969, *Ribes* was in rapid decline at the time most males left their territories, and in general those birds whose *Ribes* supply lasted longest stayed territorial longest. In 1970, *Ribes* had practically stopped blooming when observations were begun in April (fig. 13). In 1969, however, a number of birds continued to maintain breeding territories by switching to other food plants, notably *Nicotiana*. At the time when *Ribes* was in decline, other flowers were rapidly increasing. On the territory of one marked male for which I kept detailed records, the total food supply available was actually greater when he left his territory than it had been a month earlier. Thus, decline of *Ribes* supplies at best a partial answer, although it is definitely true that *Ribes speciosum* is the most nectar-rich (hence energetically favorable) food plant in the chaparral (table 1).

There remains the possibility of competition. As discussed above, *anna* males are dominant to both *alexandri* and *costae* males (table 11), and I do not think that competition from these other breeding residents was a decisive factor in breakdown of breeding territoriality in male *anna*. Even in one case where an *alexandri* male took over the same area that had been occupied by an *anna* male, the latter was still able to dominate the *alexandri* fairly consistently when he entered the area.

Migratory concentrations of *S. rufus* sometimes have a severe effect on *anna* breeding territoriality, as discussed earlier. In 1968, however, fewer *rufus* appeared in the chaparral, and they left sooner than in 1969. In each year, a burst of renewed territorial activity by most *anna* males followed the departure of these migrants, and when *anna* males finally began to go off territory, postbreeding *Selasphorus* were not yet in evidence.

As with migratory *rufus*, juvenile *anna* sometimes "swamp out" a territorial male *anna* by sheer weight of numbers. Once established on feeding territories, these juveniles may be very difficult to dislodge. A high proportion of the territorial defense of *anna* males during the latter half of the breeding season is directed against juvenile *anna*. Along the ridgetop trail at Franklin Canyon, I began seeing large numbers of juvenile *anna* in trail censuses in late March and early April 1968, but not until late April and early May of 1969. This coincides fairly well with the timing of territorial decline in both years, and it is my opinion that the effort required to defend a breeding territory against the encroachments of an increasing number of juveniles may play an important part in the final abandonment of breeding territoriality by adult male *anna*. The 1970 data neither contradict nor conclusively support this opinion; *anna* juveniles were already numerous, and breeding territory in decline, when observations were begun.

To summarize, it may be profitable to view the decline in breeding territoriality from the viewpoint of time and energy. The augmented energy drain of territorial defense against migrants, breeding residents, and most importantly, *anna* juveniles, may ultimately prove to be too great to permit the maintenance of a large territory. Seen in this light, the decline of the most energetically advantageous food flower may be especially crucial. Even though total food on a male's territory may increase, if he cannot efficiently exploit it to offset increased energy demands, his effectiveness will be decreased. Add to these factors a general decline in territorial vigor, of which the onset of molt may be a sign, one can see that it is the combination of several factors which ultimately erodes the effectiveness of a territorial male.

The important part played by *anna* juveniles is especially intriguing from a theoretical point of view. The timing of the appearance of large numbers of juveniles is a reflection of the relative nesting success of *anna* females early in the year, as a comparison of nesting in 1967-68, 1968-69, and 1969-70 clearly shows. Due to late territorial establishment of *anna* males and severe January storms in the second season, most females were unable to bring off young until April at the earliest, while many broods were successfully fledged in February and March of 1968. In 1970, some broods were fledged as early as mid-January, and many young were brought off in February and March. What we have, in effect, is a reproductive feedback system, in which the products of the system—the juveniles—help to exert a restraining influence upon further production. I emphasize that there is no need to invoke group selection to account for this phenomenon. A male *anna* attempting to maintain his territory in the face of increasing energy demands and declining resources may well incur a reduced chance of survival, and hence of reproduction in succeeding years. (The same applies to a female that expends energy in nest construction late in the year, then is unable to find a male to mate with.) In this connection, the data of Ortiz (1967) strongly suggest that a similar feedback mechanism may be operating in the population of *sasin* he studied, for he states that juvenile territoriality ultimately "overwhelms" the breeding territoriality of adult males.

The other major studies on territoriality and reproduction in *C. anna* unfortunately offer little information regarding the possibility of reproductive feedback, as outlined above. Pitelka (1951) and Williamson (1956) devoted most of their attention to male *anna* and relatively little to juveniles, which apparently did not appear in numbers on male territories. However, most of the males they studied commuted to feeding areas off territory, and they do not consider the possibility of encroachment of juvenile *anna* into feeding areas. Ortiz (1967) described the movement of juvenile *anna* into feeding areas, but did not consider the territorial behavior of adult males. Legg and Pitelka (1956) were chiefly concerned with the interspecific interactions of female *anna* and *sasin*, and did not discuss juveniles in any detail.

FOOD SUPPLY AND SEASONAL MOVEMENTS

The Anna Hummingbird engages in a great variety of population movements, from true migrations involving the bulk of the population, to local shifts between habitats by many birds, to relatively uncoordinated wanderings by individuals and perhaps small groups. In this section, I wish to examine the role of distribution of food resources, specifically flowers, in determining the direction, extent, and timing of these movements.

A number of the seasonal movements just referred to have already been discussed in previous sections. The movement of *anna* males from gardens and planted areas to breeding territories in the chaparral is dependent upon the appearance of suitable food supplies in or near the prospective breeding territories. It is certainly not occasioned by any shortage of food in the gardens, as was also emphasized by Ortiz (1967). Food shortages, in themselves, also seem inadequate to account for the fall departure of postbreeding *Selasphorus* from the Santa Monica Mountains: *Nicotiana*, their main food plant, is still in good bloom after they have left. The same is true of the departure of *Selasphorus* from the Berkeley area (Ortiz, 1967).

The nearest thing to a true migration in *anna* is the movement of the bulk of the population to the high mountains in summer. Grinnell (1908) notes that July through October are the "winter" months of food supply in the Southern California chaparral. He describes the nearly universal exodus of many bird species from the coastal lowlands and foothills at this time, most notably the hummingbirds *anna* and *alexandri*. Many summer visitants in the lowlands actually have a 3-part migration: between the wintering area, the breeding grounds, and the summer feeding grounds. Such a pattern occurs to some degree in all California hummingbirds (Grinnell and Miller, 1944). The first phase of fall migration in these birds is a very gradual southward movement down the main mountain chains of the state, covering roughly the months July to September or October. When cold weather begins to cut down the food supply at high elevations, migration "proper" begins and the birds depart swiftly for the wintering grounds (Grinnell, 1908; Grinnell and Swarth, 1913). In the Anna Hummingbird, the eastward dispersal over the deserts occurs at this time. Observers in Phoenix, Tucson, and Nogales, Arizona, inform me that *anna* are present in those areas during November and December, and that they depart sometime in late December or January—presumably to return to the breeding range (R. and J. Witzemann, W. Harrison, personal communications).

In the high mountains, such as the San Gabriel, San Bernardino, and San Jacinto ranges of Southern California, *anna* begin to appear in May (Grinnell, 1908; R. Adams, personal communication). During most of May and June, their main food flower is a manzanita, *Arctostaphylos manzanita*; according to Grinnell, by the time this plant ceases to bloom, various species of *Penstemon* are coming into full flower. By late July and August, the numbers of *anna* in the high mountains are at a maximum, and large numbers of other hummingbird species (*rufus*, *sasin*, *alexandri*, and *calliope*) are concentrated at good feeding areas as well (Grinnell, 1908; Grant and Grant, 1967 and 1968). Grinnell notes that many of these late-summer birds are fat, and this applies to *anna* as well as to the more migratory species. I have captured *anna* in the San Jacinto Mountains in September that weighed as much as 6.2 grams (males) and 5.4 grams (females), an increase of about 25 percent over their respective weights in the breeding season (cf. table 2). Grinnell (1908) stated that this fat deposition was of considerable importance in enabling Anna Hummingbirds to survive the fall period of food scarcity in the lowlands; it is probably important to those birds that disperse eastwards into the deserts as well. In neither desert nor chaparral does there appear to be much in the way of native food plants blooming in October and November, before the rains. Perhaps the original result of the dispersal movements at this season was simply to spread the population as thinly as possible, so as not to exhaust the food resources of any one area. It is even possible that originally the entire *anna* population wintered in northwestern Mexico, where suitable flowers are available at this time of year. However, as will be discussed below, man has changed the distribution of food so radically that the original condition will probably never be known.

GEOGRAPHIC VARIATION IN THE ANNUAL CYCLE OF THE ANNA HUMMINGBIRD

The most comprehensive body of reliable information available for comparison is the work of Pitelka and his associates on *anna* in the San Francisco Bay region (Pitelka, 1951a; Legg and Pitelka, 1956; Williamson 1956; Ortiz, 1967). This area, some 300 miles northwest of the Santa Monica Mountains, has a considerably cooler and wetter climate (cf. Williamson, 1956; fig. 8 on p. 363). The Allen Hummingbird breeds there, but Costa and Black-chinned Hummingbirds do not. Nearly all of their observations were made in man-created or man-influenced habitats—botanical gardens, *Eucalyptus* groves, etc. My results may not be fully equatable with theirs in all respects, but the resulting comparisons give a fairly well-balanced picture of the ecology of *anna* over the major part of its breeding range.

There appears to be geographic variation in the initiation of breeding between Los Angeles and Berkeley. Certain major differences between Williamson's (1956) observations and mine could be explained by differences in the time at which the birds became photosensitive in the two populations we studied. Williamson mentions that "substantial" rains during the first half of November did not result in breeding territoriality, and that males with fully mature testes were not seen until early to mid-December. Such rains would almost certainly have induced breeding territoriality in Anna Hummingbirds of the Santa Monica Mountains, where males with greatly enlarged testes were collected following moderate rains in mid-November (fig. 8). It is also possible that, in the normally much wetter conditions of Berkeley, the threshold for response to rainfall is higher than in the population I studied.

A striking difference in the timing of the decline of breeding territoriality, and in the onset of molt, is evident between the Los Angeles and Berkeley populations. According to Pitelka (1951a) and Williamson (1956), territorial behavior in male *anna* at Berkeley begins to subside in late May and early June. Williamson found that display and song ceased by mid-June in most areas, and that the annual molt in most adults began in early June. These events occur between

1 and 2 months earlier in the Los Angeles population. Nesting activity in *anna* females also continues much later in northern populations, as at Santa Cruz (Legg and Pitelka, 1956), some 50 miles south of Berkeley. Interestingly enough, the egg dates cited by Pitelka (1951b) for the geographically and climatically intermediate Santa Barbara region suggest that the *anna* breeding season there is also more or less intermediate in timing.

There is some disagreement regarding how long male *anna* defend their breeding territories at Berkeley. Pitelka (1951a) asserted that some male *anna* defended the core areas of their territories year-round, but his evidence for this is questionable, especially as food supply was not mentioned. The observations of Williamson (1956), and Ortiz (1967), who found that most *anna* males held feeding territories between July and November, are much more in line with my own. However, if *anna* males at Berkeley do not defend their breeding territories through the summer, they certainly abandon them less abruptly than do *anna* males at Los Angeles, and may occupy if not defend some part of these territories through July or even August (Pitelka, 1951a).

INFLUENCE OF MAN ON THE ANNUAL CYCLE OF THE ANNA HUMMINGBIRD

There are any number of ways in which man can, directly or indirectly, alter the population biology of a species. Perhaps the most widespread effects stem from his alteration of natural habitats, and this alteration has been very extensive on the coastal slope of Southern California. However, habitat alteration per se has probably affected hummingbird populations of this area less than has man's introduction of potential food plants from all over the world. The result of this has been to drastically change the spatial and temporal distribution of flowers available for utilization by *anna* and other California hummingbirds. This has had far-reaching effects on hummingbird distribution, numbers, and movements, both locally and over large areas.

For the Anna Hummingbird, the most significant human activity has been the introduction of such fall-blooming plants as *Nicotiana* and *Eucalyptus*. By effectively increasing the carrying capacity of the habitat at a crucial period of the year, when virtually no native flowers are blooming, man has unquestionably increased the total Anna Hummingbird population greatly (cf. Grinnell and Miller, 1944). Locally, the presence of introduced food plants such as *Eucalyptus* may enable chaparral areas to support territorial male *anna*, that might otherwise have been marginal or unavailable due to lack of suitable food plants. Because of the steep slopes and unstable substrate, chaparral areas generally are unsuitable for house-building purposes (as the winter rains demonstrate annually), and most of the actual habitat alteration in the Santa Monica Mountains has occurred in the oak woodlands of the canyon bottoms. In many cases, the original oaks and sycamores are left standing, and the planting of introduced flowers may greatly increase the attractiveness of such areas for nesting female *anna*.

The ability of introduced food plants to increase the density of nesting female *anna* is shown by the fact that, in any given year, there were 2 to 3 times as many nests in Stone Canyon as in Trancas (fig. 6). The areas censused in the two canyons were approximately 10 and 12 hectares in extent, respectively. I would estimate that I found about 70 percent of the nests in each area, judging from the proportions of females showing signs of nesting activity whose nests I actually located. Of particular interest at Stone Canyon is the "garden grove" area (plate 3B) a 1½-hectare oak-alder-redwood grove with a planted understory of *Fuchsia, Abutilon, Heliconia, Jacobinia,* and several other flowers used intensively by hummingbirds. In this area, physiognomically fairly similar to the oak-sycamore woodland at Trancas, I found 25 nests in the two years, more than in the entire area of Trancas Canyon!

Despite the great differences in density of nests, nesting success of *anna* was similar in Stone and Trancas Canyons, and comparable to that found by other authors for *anna* and *costae* (table 10). The slightly higher success at Stone may have reflected more abundant food and/or lower predation. Potential avian predators (jays, orioles, mockingbirds, etc.) were no less common than at Trancas, and human disturbance was definitely greater. Snakes, however, were much less abundant at Stone Canyon. Skutch (1966) and others report that nesting success of open-nesting birds, including hummingbirds, is higher in man-made habitats than in natural ones, largely because of the relative scarcity of snakes. Nesting success of *alexandri* in man-made habitats was the same as or lower than that in natural ones (table 10), perhaps due to differences in nest camouflage (see above).

Man has apparently had no major effects on the timing of breeding in *anna*. In spite of the availability of blooming *Eucalyptus* trees at Stone Canyon, male *anna* did not take up breeding territories until after the first heavy winter rains, at about the same time as in other chaparral areas. During both 1968 and 1969, nesting activity of female *anna* began slightly sooner at Stone Canyon than at Trancas (fig. 6). This I attribute to the fact that *anna* females at Trancas did not start nesting until *Ribes malvaceum* began to bloom in the canyon bottom, whereas at Stone flowers were continuously available (cf. fig. 4).

In a similar manner, I doubt that man has greatly affected the timing of seasonal movements in *anna*, but that he has very probably reduced the proportion of the population that does move. During the summer and early fall, the only places where *anna* is found in the Santa Monica Mountains area are gardens and planted areas. It seems fairly likely that, before man created such habitats, virtually the entire population migrated to the high mountains in summer, and dispersed over the desert in fall.

Most of the other California hummingbirds have probably been affected by man in much the same ways as has *anna*, though perhaps in somewhat lesser degree. Certainly the postbreeding concentrations of *Selasphorus* at *Nicotiana* patches in the coastal lowlands would scarcely have been present; doubtless the entire populations of *sasin* and *rufus* would have moved southward down the mountains during the summer rather than, in part, along the coastal slope. Large numbers of *alexandri* and *sasin* breed in gardens and other areas where man has augmented the food supply, much as does *anna* (cf. Dawson, 1923; Ortiz, 1967). Man has increased the amount of food available along migration routes, most notably by his planting of citrus orchards (cf. Woods, 1927, 1940), and has probably decreased the mortality of various species during migration. In all probability the two species least affected by man have been *calliope* and *costae*. Both breed in areas where the influence of man has been less extensive: high mountain meadows, and dry chaparral and desert, respectively. In the Santa Monica Mountains, *costae* is the only species not to make extensive use of man-made habitats such as gardens. This may reflect its preference for dry, open areas, or its subordinate status relative to *anna* and *alexandri* (table 11), which do concentrate in these habitats. Even so, *costae* does feed abundantly on *Nicotiana* during the summer. In the desert, where no other hummers breed, *costae* may be found around gardens and plantings. Thus, virtually every species of California hummingbird has probably benefited by the influence of man (see also Grinnell and Miller, 1944). Whether this influence will continue to be favorable, is another question.

The Evolution of Winter Breeding in the Anna Hummingbird

A brief survey of the seasonal distributions of growth and reproduction in other chaparral organisms will help to place the annual cycle of the Anna Hummingbird in its proper ecological context, and will set the stage for a discussion of evolutionary aspects of the timing of breeding in *C. anna*.

GROWTH AND REPRODUCTIVE SEASONS OF OTHER CHAPARRAL ORGANISMS

Plants.—As discussed earlier, growth and flowering of most chaparral plants is inhibited by lack of moisture in late summer and fall, and by low temperatures in winter (Miller, 1947). A number of summer-deciduous chaparral shrubs (e.g., *Ribes* spp., *Salvia* spp., *Diplacus*, *Encelia*, etc.) respond to the winter rains with a flush of new leaves. Flowering may begin at the same time as vegetative growth (*Ribes malvaceum*), within a few weeks (*R. speciosum*), or not until months later (*Salvia*, *Diplacus*, etc.). Most evergreen chaparral shrubs commence vegetative growth in late winter or early spring (Miller, 1957; Hanes, 1965). A few herbaceous plants, especially grasses, sprout or leaf out following the winter rains, but again most species commence growth in spring. The vast majority of chaparral plants flowers in the spring; in the Santa Monica Mountains, May and June are the months of peak blooming activity for the chaparral as a whole (fig. 3). During the coldest winter months, practically the only plants in bloom are *Ribes* spp., and *Arctostaphylos* (which is evergreen and produces new leaves in spring). Fruit ripens on most chaparral shrubs during the summer and early fall.

Insects.—Extremely little is known about the annual cycles of chaparral insects. Unpublished studies by M. L. Cody and R. Yeaton represent the only data available on seasonal changes in overall insect abundance and biomass in the chaparral, and form the basis for the following discussion. The peak of insect abundance comes in late spring and early summer, roughly coinciding with the peak of flowering of chaparral plants. Following a rapid decline in late summer, insect abundance increases, and over the winter fluctuates widely but generally remains rather low (M. L. Cody, R. Yeaton, unpublished data). I emphasize that these data apply mainly to flying insects, and that they may not hold true within particular taxonomic groups.

Reptiles and amphibians.—Most chaparral reptiles hibernate during the cold winter months, and emerge and breed with the warmer temperatures and increased insect abundance of spring. Many chaparral amphibians, on the other hand, commence breeding or other activity with the winter rains, following a period of estivation during the hot, dry fall weather. Chorusing in the frogs *Rana aurora* and *Hyla regilla* and the toad *Bufo boreas*, and oviposition in the salamander *Batrachoseps attenuatus*, are triggered by the onset of the winter rains (Stebbins, 1951). The rains stimulate migratory activity in the newt *Taricha torosa*, but breeding does not take place until spring (Pimentel, 1960).

Birds.—The Anna Hummingbird is the only chaparral bird that regularly begins breeding before the winter solstice. The next species to begin nesting is probably the Great Horned Owl, for which the earliest known California egg date is 29 January (Skinner, 1938; Dawson, 1923). Most chaparral birds feed their young at least partly on insects, and so tend to breed in spring when the latter are most abundant. Fall and winter breeding are probably inhibited by food shortages and inclement weather. Erickson (1938) found that the cold months of December through February were the time of greatest mortality, and greatest attraction to artificial feeding stations, in the population of Wrentits (*Chamaea fasciata*) she studied.

Most resident chaparral birds begin to breed in February, March, or April. In the Brown Towhee (*Pipilo fuscus*), territorial defense starts in late fall (Childs, 1968). Several species that are territorial year-round may be stimulated to sing by the winter rains. Examples include the California Thrasher, *Toxostoma redivivum* (Woods, 1948) and the Bewick Wren, *Thryomanes bewickii* (Miller, 1941). In very mild years, the rains may stimulate *Toxostoma* to breed as early as November (Sargent, 1940), but its breeding season normally begins in February or March (Woods, 1948). The cold weather following the winter rains is the time of least singing activity in *Chamaea fasciata*, another species that is territorial year-round (Erickson, 1938).

Mammals.—The only study of annual cycles of chaparral mammals is that of MacMillen (1964) on the rodent fauna of a more inland "semidesert" locality. In climate and vegetation, this locality appears fairly comparable to the warmer and drier parts of the Santa Monica Mountains. MacMillen found that March through May was the peak of reproduction for all mammal species studied. *Peromyscus eremicus* and *maniculatus* apparently produced young year-round, but other species had well-defined breeding seasons. *Neotoma lepida* began to breed in November, and it seems not unlikely that the winter rains, directly or indirectly, stimulate breeding in this species (and perhaps in the congeneric *fuscipes* as well) although this possibility was not considered by MacMillen. The other species of the area commenced breeding in January and February. The most stressful period for most species appeared to be the hot, dry late summer and fall months. A major factor in the decline in population of most rodent species at this time was water shortage, occasioned by the monopolizing of good stands of succulent vegetation by the large, aggressive *Neotoma lepida*. Unfortunately, MacMillen made no detailed observations on food habits, and his statement that there was no scarcity of food at any time of year appears to be unsupported by concrete data. Certainly the relationship between food supply and the winter rains bears further study.

In conclusion, the timing of breeding in the Anna Hummingbird is unique among chaparral birds. The midwinter shortage of insects and fruit may affect *anna* less than it does other birds. The Anna's small size and consequently lower total food requirement may be a preadaptation for breeding when food is scarce. Also, I have gained the strong subjective impression that the very small insects eaten by *anna* may be less affected by the winter cold than are larger insects, in terms of numbers and activity. Even in the coldest months, I have seen swarms of small dipterans in oak woodland and chaparral—complete with avidly-hawking hummingbirds! Most important of all, in *Ribes* nectar the Anna Hummingbird has a rich energy source not available to other chaparral birds. Birds much larger than a hummingbird would be unable to obtain sufficient food from *Ribes* to appreciably affect their energy balance, while the tubular shape of the flowers makes it difficult for other small—but short-billed—birds (e.g., the Bushtit, *Psaltriparus minimus*) to reach the nectar. In short, I believe that the ability to efficiently exploit nectar as well as insects is the most important single factor enabling *anna* to breed during the winter. The evolutionary implications of this situation will be discussed in the next section.

Among other chaparral vertebrates, the initiation of breeding appears closely correlated with the winter rains only in amphibians (and perhaps certain mammals). In amphibians, water itself is necessary for reproduction, and in general amphibians can operate much more effectively at low temperatures than can reptiles (Stebbins, 1951), so that winter breeding is feasible. Certain mammals, notably *Neotoma*, deserve further study in this connection. I would predict the direct stimulus for breeding is the flush of new leaves and grass following the winter rains. This situation would then be more comparable to that in the Anna Hummingbird, in which food supply also plays a major role in stimulating reproduction.

TIMING OF BREEDING IN THE ANNA HUMMINGBIRD: ULTIMATE FACTORS

The ultimate control of avian breeding seasons can generally be explained in terms of food supply, the eggs being laid during a period which anticipates the season when food for the young is most readily available (Thomson, 1950). In the Anna Hummingbird, this appears to be the case, although it may not provide the entire answer. In most years, the earliest young fledge in late January and early February, when *Ribes speciosum* is rapidly increasing in blooming activity and *R. malvaceum* is not yet in full decline. Most broods of *anna* fledge between about March and June. *Ribes speciosum* reaches its peak in March, and by the time it has ceased to flower a wide variety of other potential food flowers (table 1; fig. 3) are approaching full bloom. The weather has warmed up, and insects are abundant—in short, the chaparral food supply is at its maximum. Young fledging much later than this must contend with declining food supplies and increasingly stressful climatic conditions.

The early breeding of Anna Hummingbirds may give them an advantage in competition with other chaparral hummingbirds. Pitelka (1951a) notes that *anna* males at Berkeley set up breeding territories in *sasin* habitat before the latter arrive in the spring, and that they are usually able to prevent *sasin* from settling in such areas, probably because of the psychological advantage of prior territorial residence. In the Santa Monica Mountains, the dominance of *anna* males over those of *alexandri* and *costae* may be enhanced in this way. Perhaps more important, however, is the fact that early nesting enables juvenile *anna*, with their precocious territoriality, to obtain control of feeding areas in the chaparral before the other residents arrive. Once in control of such feeding areas, young *anna* may become dominant to other birds, such as male *alexandri* (see above), that are normally dominant to them. The presence of large numbers of juvenile *anna* in the chaparral by early March 1968 may be one reason why relatively few *rufus* were seen in the chaparral that year.

The early (relative to other chaparral hummingbirds) cessation of breeding in *anna* has already been considered in relation to male breeding territoriality. A further selective force against late nesting may be provided by the apparently reduced chance of reproductive success by young male *anna* fledged very late in the year. Most observers who have studied *anna* extensively have found that some first-year males are extremely late in completing the postjuvenal molt, and may not settle on a breeding territory until several weeks or even months after most adult males have done so (Pitelka, 1951a; Williamson, 1956; Ortiz, 1967; and present study). I suspect that such individuals may not breed at all during the first year. A young male *anna* held a feeding territory at a large *Cestrum* bush at Stone Canyon continuously between early December 1968 and late March 1969. When first discovered, the bird had a sprinkling of red feathers on crown and gorget and white-tipped rectrices; the date precludes his being a product of the 1968-69 breeding season. The bird's plumage did not change appreciably during the period I watched him, though his song became quite mature-sounding. This bird was most likely the product of a late nesting during the 1967-68 breeding season, and almost certainly did not obtain a territory until the 1969-70 season, assuming he survived that long. If this situation is general in young *anna* fledged late in the year, it should provide strong selection against late nestings.

COEVOLUTION OF REPRODUCTIVE SEASONS IN *Calypte anna* AND *Ribes speciosum*

Ribes and *Arctostaphylos* depart from the seasonal reproductive pattern of most chaparral plants in exactly the same way as does *anna* from that of most chaparral birds. Most spring-blooming chaparral plants are pollinated by insects, whereas *Ribes speciosum* is exclusively hummingbird-pollinated, and *R. malvaceum* and *Arctostaphylos* are apparently transitional between insect and hummingbird pollination (the "bill-tip pollination" of Grant and Grant, 1968). During the coldest winter months, *Ribes speciosum* is thus as dependent on *anna* for pollination as *anna* is on *speciosum* for food: winter reproduction in either species would be impossible without the other. This great degree of ecological interdependence strongly suggests that winter breeding in the two taxa evolved together. The benefits gained by *speciosum* from early breeding are probably analogous to those gained by *anna*: a longer reproductive season, and avoidance of competition for pollinators and perhaps for dispersal agents as well.

Grant and Grant (1968) argue convincingly that flowers specialized for pollination by hummingbirds evolved from bee-pollinated forms. The key evolutionary question is, under what ecological conditions will hummingbird pollination be more advantageous than the ancestral bee pollination? The *anna-speciosum* interaction functions most effectively during the coldest months of the year. Cold depresses insect activity in general, and it is my strong subjective impression that bees are much scarcer in the chaparral during the winter months than in the spring. Hummingbirds, on the other hand, must feed more during cold weather (Stiles, 1971a and unpublished observations), and their value as pollinating agents is enhanced at these times. The abundant nectar produced by *speciosum* enhances its food value to *anna*, especially during cold weather; red flower coloration doubtless helps to attract the birds to the plant (Grant and Grant, 1968 and many others).

Sharing of the Anna Hummingbird as a pollinator may be producing some interesting evolutionary interactions between *Ribes speciosum* and *malvaceum*. Morphologically, *malvaceum* is much less specialized for hummingbird pollination then is *speciosum*, and its association with *anna* is probably a considerably more recent one. I suspect that *malvaceum* was originally pollinated by fall-flying bees that were most active before cold winter weather set in. For reasons discussed above, it was probably advantageous for *anna* to begin breeding as early in the winter as suitable flowers became available. Bloooming of *malvaceum* immediately after the start of the rains provided *anna* with a potential food source that enabled it to breed even earlier than *speciosum* could flower. Currently the times of peak flowering of the two *Ribes* species are offset by about 2 months, probably a result of competition for *anna* as a pollinator. In any such competition, the much more nectar-rich *speciosum* is probably at an advantage. It is thus unlikely that *malvaceum* will be able to extend its blooming season later, although it is perhaps possible for *speciosum* to bloom earlier. However, the early flowering of *malvaceum* is not without its hazards: in some years the burst of flowering following early rains is killed off by a hot, dry spell afterwards. This occurred in the fall of 1968 (see above), and many *malvaceum* bushes never flowered vigorously or produced fruit that year. The risk of early blooming, plus perhaps competition for pollinators from *malvaceum*, may select against earlier flowering by *speciosum*.

Food Supply and the Evolution of Breeding Territoriality

Competition among *anna* males seeking breeding territories is much more intense for sites with a good *Ribes* supply than for sites without *Ribes*, as has been discussed above. In addition to being more favorable from an energetic point of view, territories containing *Ribes* may be more advantageous as mating stations.

Contact between the sexes during courtship is brief, and in my experience is typically initiated by the female flying to the male's territory: I have no data suggesting that male *anna* seek out females. This being so, the question is: What attracts the female to a given male's territory? Or, by what criteria does a female choose the male she will mate with? One possibility is that some quality of the male himself provides the stimulus: volume or persistence of song, brighter plumage, or whatever—in short, sexual selection in the commonly understood sense. In the absence of drastic mutations, one must suppose that the differences between the various males in a population will be fairly small, very likely too small to be easily apparent to a human observer. This explanation would therefore be difficult or impossible to test.

A female may, however, choose a male, directly or indirectly, on the basis of some quality of the territory he controls—specifically, the amount of food thereon. Were the primary attractant still the male himself, then controlling a territory with a food supply would be advantageous if only because the male would need to leave his territory less, and would be more likely to be present should a female present herself. It is also possible that the food itself is the primary attractant. On this view, contact between the sexes should be initiated by a female's attempting to feed in a male's territory—and the male controlling the best food supply should attract the most females.

There is considerable circumstantial evidence to support this view. I have on many occasions seen females enter a male's territory, begin to feed, and get chased. However, courtship chases in *anna* are often lengthy, and copulations do not, in my experience, take place on the males' territory. Hence, it is impossible to tell if the chases so initiated ended in copulations. There is evidence that males controlling more *Ribes* engage in more and longer chases in territorial defense (table 9). Unfortunately, it is frequently impossible to identify the bird chased before the male drives it off. Although some of a male's longer absences may begin in a chase, one has no guarantee that the bird is chasing (or mating) during the time he is out of contact.

If female *anna* do tend to mate with the male that controls the best food supply, then the most important quality of the male himself will be his proficiency in territorial defense. The proximate agents of selection will thus be the other males with whom he competes for a territory. As competition for territories containing good food resources is more intense, it follows that the males that finally control such territories will be competitively superior to other males. These males may, in turn, sire the most vigorous progeny, and a female might effectively maximize her own reproductive potential by mating with such a male. In this manner, selection may favor those females who visit males with superior territories.

As Huxley (1938), Selander (1965), and Orians (1969) have noted, the term "sexual selection" has been frequently used to describe both epigamic (intersexual) and intrasexual selection. Pitelka (1942) and Wolf (1969) suggested that many of the striking displays and plumage characteristics of male hummingbirds evolved because of their importance in territorial defense, rather than in mate selection per se. Wolf and I believe that this phenomenon should be distinguished from sexual (epigamic) selection, and we have proposed the name "aggressive selection" for it (Wolf and Stiles, 1970). In *Calypte anna* then, the quality of the food supply on a male's territory is in effect a secondary sexual characteristic, to which females may respond (cf. Selander, 1965). The basis for this kind of mating system in *anna* is provided by the patchy, irregular dispersion of flowers especially *Ribes*; this enables different males to control very different amounts of food even though the variation in territory size is relatively slight.

In this connection, Pitelka (1942) has asserted that the mating function of the territories of male hummingbirds is secondary or derived, and that the primary function, in an evolutionary sense, is the defense of a food supply. The breeding territories of many North American hummingbirds are still centered about a food supply (see Saunders, 1936; Pitelka, 1942; Bene, 1946; Ortiz, 1967; and beyond). In effect, the progression between feeding and breeding territoriality in *C. anna* may correspond to an evolutionary, as well as ecological, sequence!

DISCUSSION

In this section I will compare the biology of the Anna Hummingbird with that of other hummingbirds, and with nectar-feeding birds in general. My main objective is to identify and discuss some of the ecological and behavioral correlates of nectar-feeding, especially with respect to breeding, seasonal movements, territoriality, and mating system. Correlations of this sort are discussed for a wide variety of birds in the stimulating analyses of Crook (1965) and Lack (1968). However, neither of these authors pays specific attention to nectarivorous birds, or to the properties of flowers as a food resource.

The most important ecological characteristic of floral food sources is their extremely patchy, localized distribution, in both space and time. Suitable flowers seldom cover large areas evenly, and blooming seasons are short in relation to the annual cycle, and to the life-span of nectar-feeding birds. Therefore, movement between patches is a necessity, in both space and time. Flowers are stationary and conspicuous, so that once their location is learned, birds can return periodically to check for blooming with minimal wasted effort. For the same reasons, flowers can be exploited with a minimum of energy expended in searching out individual food items. This, plus their highly localized distribution, makes flowers energetically profitable for territorial birds to defend (cf. Brown, 1964).

As discussed above, various features of the biology of the Anna Hummingbird can be related to the patchy distribution of flowers in space and time. The following discussion attempts to determine to what extent these correlations hold in other nectar-feeding birds.

Food Supply, Breeding, and Seasonal Movements of Nectar-Feeding Birds

The flowering seasons of important food plants, rather than abundance of insects, is the factor most strongly correlated with breeding seasonality in most hummingbirds for which such data exist. Skutch (1950) notes that in Central America, hummingbirds and the highly nectarivorous flower-piercer *Diglossa baritula* bring off young at the season when flowers are most abundant. In Trinidad, Snow and Snow (1964) found that hummingbirds and the highly nectarivorous coerebid *Coereba flaveola* brought off young when their respective favorite flowers were abundant. The same appears to hold for many South African sunbirds (Skead, 1967), and the sugarbirds *Promerops cafer* and *P. gurneyi* (Broekhuysen, 1959; Skead, 1963). The breeding season of *Promerops cafer* is different in different regions, apparently correlated with the flowering seasons of the dominant species of *Protea* in the respective areas (Winterbottom, 1962; see also Broekhuysen, 1963).

A complementary situation is found in the sunbirds *Nectarinia kilimensis* and *N. purpureiventris* in the highlands of equatorial Africa. These sunbirds are very closely associated with the flowers of *Erythrina* and *Symphonia* trees, respectively. Each individual of these tree species has its own more-or-less annual blooming period, but different individuals are not synchronized and at any time of the year, some trees can be found in flower. A parallel situation exists in the sunbirds: breeding pairs can be found year-round, but different pairs breed at different times. This is in contrast to most birds of the region which have discrete breeding seasons associated with the annual wet-dry climatic cycle (Chapin, 1959).

A number of hummingbird species resemble *C. anna* in breeding at the coldest and/or wettest time of year, in marked contrast to the rest of the local avifauna. Examples include *Panterpe insignis* (Wolf and Stiles, 1970), *Colibri thalassinus* (Wagner, 1945), *Hylocharis leucotis* (Moore, 1939), *Phaethornis* spp. (Skutch, 1964), and several Central American highland species (Skutch, 1967). As these are also the times when insect pollination might be least advantageous, one would expect to find a rather close ecological correspondence between the breeding of the hummingbirds and the blooming of some important food plant. Relationships similar to that between *C. anna* and *Ribes speciosum* may exist between *Panterpe insignis* and *Macleania glabra* (Wolf and Stiles, 1970), *Colibri thalassinus* and *Salvia* spp. (Wagner, 1945), and *Phaethornis* spp. and *Heliconia* spp. (Stiles, unpublished observations), among others.

The cooler climates of highland areas make bird pollination frequently more advantageous than insect pollination, and ornithophilous flowers are numerous in many montane regions. Conversely, the greatest ecological and taxonomic diversity among the hummingbirds occurs in the Andes of Colombia, Ecuador, and Peru (cf. Chapman, 1926: 131). The highly nectarivorous coerebid genera *Conirostrum* and *Diglossa* also achieve their greatest diversity in this region (Chapman, 1926; Vuilleumier, 1969). In the mountains of Africa, sunbirds are very well represented at high elevations (e.g., Chapin, 1932 and 1954). In South Africa, such nectar feeders as *Promerops* and various sunbirds are characteristic of highlands and mountain slopes (Broekhuysen, 1959; Skead, 1963 and 1967; Snell, 1963). The relatively high energy needs of birds living at high altitudes is reflected in the extremely close ecological associations between many highland nectar feeders and important food flowers. Among the hummingbirds, examples include *Panterpe* and *Macleania*, and *Colibri* and *Salvia* (see above); *Oreotrochilus chimborazo* and *Chuquiraga acutifolia* (Smith, 1969); *Sappho sparganura* and *Dunalia brachyacanthia* (Contino, in litt.); *Selasphorus flammula* and *Castilleja irasuensis* (Stiles, unpublished observations); and doubtless many others. In Africa the associations between *Promerops* spp. and *Protea* spp. (Broekhuysen,

1959; Skead, 1963), various sunbirds and *Aloe* spp. (Skead, 1967), and *Nectarinia johnstoni* and lobelias (Chapin, 1954) might be mentioned.

In many species of hummingbirds, the distribution of flowers has been found to influence the location of the females' nesting effort. Legg and Pitelka (1956) mention that the *Eucalyptus* trees in which *C. anna* and *Selasphorus sasin* nested also served as their main food source. The distribution of *Archilochus colubris* nests was found to be polarized about stands of *Monarda didyma* by Saunders (1936). Similar relationships have been thought to hold for many other hummers: *Colibri thalassinus* (Wagner, 1945), *Oreotrochilus* spp. (Smith, 1969), *Panterpe insignis* (Wolf and Stiles, 1970), *Aphantochroa cirrhochloris* (Ruschi, 1950), to name a few. In general, it would appear that localized or patchy nectar resources (or feeders) usually result in a correspondingly localized distribution of nesting by female hummingbirds. A comparable degree of localization may occur about *Symphonia* trees in the sunbird *Nectarinia purpureiventris* (Chapin, 1959).

I know of no published data comparable to that for *C. anna* regarding the importance of flowers as a proximate stimulus for breeding. Similar responses to flowers and/or rainfall might be expected in other nectar-feeders of dry areas, such as certain Australian honeyeaters (Keast, 1968) or African sunbirds (Skead, 1967). Also worthy of study in this respect are the hummingbirds of the more arid areas of southern South America; much of this region is climatically and floristically strikingly similar to the deserts and chaparral of California.

Virtually every nectar-feeding bird whose annual cycle has been studied in any detail has been found to undertake some kind of seasonal movements related, at least in part, to changes in the distribution and availability of flowers. I think it likely that, as a group, nectar feeders are among the most nomadic of small land birds. As in the Anna Hummingbird, these movements seem to occur mostly outside the breeding season. Anywhere from a few individuals to an entire population may be involved, and the movement may be local or regional, random or directed, brief or protracted.

The postbreeding movement of *anna* and other California hummingbirds into the high mountains has already been mentioned. This concentration of hummingbirds in the mountains is matched by the abundance and variety of hummingbird-pollinated flowers blooming there in late summer (Grant and Grant, 1967). Similar altitudinal movements and postbreeding hummingbird concentrations occur in the mountains of southern Arizona and New Mexico (Bent, 1940; Bene, 1946). Altitudinal movements are known in various African sunbirds, largely in response to blooming of such food plants as *Aloe* (Snell, 1963; Skead, 1967; see also Chapin, 1954). *Promerops* spp. typically descend from their mountainside breeding areas when the *Protea* cease blooming there, and may visit cultivated flowers at this time (Broekhuysen, 1959; Skead, 1963).

In tropical hummingbirds, information on seasonal movements is scanty due to the paucity of long-term observations. Skutch (1967) has amassed some information on Central American highland species, and Wagner (1945) has traced the movements of *Colibri thalassinus* in Mexico; he states that migration is dependent upon food supplies and weather. Ruschi (1967) has enumerated a number of migratory species in Brazil, but gives no supporting data. There are numerous records in the literature of drastic seasonal changes in abundance of various tropical hummers at particular localities (e.g., Wolf, 1970; Stiles and Wolf, 1970), but the migration patterns remain unknown. However, in each well-studied case, a hummingbird's presence in a given area corresponded with the blooming season of certain important food plants (e.g., Wolf, 1969 and 1970).

On the local level, many observers have stated that movements of hummingbirds occur in response to shifts in the distribution of flowers. The data in the present study from the reservoir censuses (table 6) provide a typical example. Of particular interest in this connection are the data of Ruschi (1949) on the extent of local movements and individual foraging ranges of several Brazilian species. He recaptured a *Melanothochilus fuscus* at *Eucalyptus* flowers just 10 hours after banding it at a blooming *Genipa* tree 30 kilometers away. A banded *Cytolaema rubricauda* was recaptured 2½ years later within a few meters of the original site; half an hour later, it was recaptured at still another group of flowers 2 kilometers away. Ruschi thus believes that several species of Brazilian hummingbirds may, on a daily basis, visit flower sources considerable distances apart, at least outside of the breeding season.

Nectar-feeding birds on other continents have also been found to be great wanderers, and their peregrinations ascribed to changes in distribution of flowers, over both local and long distances. Keast (1968) states that among the Australian Meliphagidae, nectarivorous species move about more than insectivorous ones. He emphasizes the nomadic nature of many of these movements, due to the sporadic, irregular, and/or nonannual flowering of many food plants, such as *Eucalyptus* (see fig. 4). He also draws a broad inverse correlation between amount and reliability of rainfall and extent of seasonal movements, noting that drier regions tend to have more sporadic and localized flowering. The wanderings of certain species of meliphagids are very closely tied to the blooming of particular food plants: for instance, *Myzomela nigra* moves about according to the flowering of the Emu Bush, *Eremophila longiflora* (Hobbs, 1958; see also Keast, 1968; Gannon, 1962; Hobbs, 1961).

A similar pattern obtains in the South African sunbirds discussed by Skead (1967). He notes that many sunbirds, especially those of dry country, are incessant wanderers and keep on the move until a nectar source is found. The birds may travel singly, in pairs, family groups, or flocks, and may concentrate in great numbers at rich nectar sources (see also Van Someren, 1956).

AGGRESSIVENESS, TERRITORIALITY, AND MATING SYSTEMS OF NECTARIVOROUS BIRDS

Many flowers are required to satisfy the daily energy requirements of a single bird. Since floral food sources are also by nature patchy and localized, there is likely to be intense competition for food among nectarivorous birds at clumps of flowers. Moreover, there are relatively few instances of exclusion of some birds from flowers because of morphological disparities between bill and corolla—for instance, most California hummingbirds have bills of fairly similar lengths (table 2). Birds with bills too short to reach the nectary via the front of the corolla tube are often able to enter the flower by puncturing the base (cf. Skead, 1967; de Carvalho, 1958; Skutch, 1954; and many others). For these reasons, most or all of the nectar-feeding birds of an area are potential direct competitors for food, regardless of species or sex. It is therefore not surprising that as a group, nectar-feeders show the greatest amount of intra- and interspecific aggressiveness at food sources of any small land birds.

There are numerous examples in the literature of interspecific competition for food being mediated by overt aggression, even including actual fighting, between individuals of different species of nectarivorous birds. Such aggression is especially well documented in the hummingbirds (see review in Stiles and Wolf, 1970; also Contino, MS; Wolf and Stiles, 1970). Sunbirds in Africa have long been known for their aggressiveness at flowers (Van Someren, 1956; Chapin, 1959; Skead, 1967; and many others). Interspecific aggression between sugarbirds (*Promerops*) and sunbirds has been described by Skead (1963). In the East Indies, aggression between sunbirds and honeyeaters at flowers is discussed by Ripley (1959). Certain Australian honeyeaters are noted for their pugnacity toward other species at flowers (Serventy and Whittell, 1951; Gannon, 1962).

Interspecific dominance hierarchies frequently result when several species of nectar-feeding birds occur at a common food source. In the present study, males of *anna* were dominant to those of *alexandri* who in turn dominated male *costae* at common feeding areas (see above and table 11). Other examples involving hummingbirds are discussed by Stiles and Wolf (1970), and a comparable case in sunbirds is described by Skead (1967); the phenomenon is doubtless widespread. A notable evolutionary result of interspecific competition and aggression is the complex mutual avoidance behaviors of certain Andean coerebids (Moynihan, 1963).

Feeding territoriality, the defense of flowers by individuals, is widespread and well documented in hummingbirds (see review by Stiles and Wolf, 1970; also Wolf, 1970; Ortiz, 1967; and present study). Van Someren (1956) describes apparently very comparable feeding territoriality in males of the sunbirds *Nectarinia famosa* and *N. kilimensis*. This report is noteworthy in that it is the only unequivocal description of feeding territoriality in any nectar-feeding bird except hummingbirds. Even allowing for the paucity of ecological studies on most other nectar-feeders, from the observations that do exist one is forced to the conclusion that feeding territoriality is rare or lacking in most groups of nectar-feeding passerines. Hummingbirds appear to be much less social, much more individualistic in their feeding behavior than do nectarivorous passerines of all kinds. Moreover, the same is true of the mating behavior and social systems of hummingbirds, relative to passerine nectar-feeders.

The mating system of *Calypte anna* is fairly typical of hummingbirds: promiscuous, with fleeting contact between the sexes only during mating itself, and with the female alone carrying on the nesting effort. Any other contacts between male and female are usually aggressive in nature (see above and Pitelka, 1942). This highly individualistic social organization appears to be the evolutionary result of dependence on such a patchy, localized, economically defensible food source as flowers, during the breeding season. Moreover, when the dispersion of the food supply is such that different males can control widely varying amounts of food, it is likely that the quality of a male's territory will be an important factor in mate choice by females. A major component of the reproductive fitness of male hummingbirds will thus be effectiveness in territorial defense, and attributes that enhance territorial effectiveness will be selected for. I therefore suspect that aggressive selection, as discussed above, has been the main force in the evolution of many secondary sexual characteristics of male hummingbirds of the genera *Calypte*, *Archilochus*, and *Selasphorus*, and perhaps for sexually dimorphic hummingbirds in general.

For example, in the Costa Hummingbird, when floral food supplies are highly localized and mostly controlled by territorial males, females may nest within the territories of such males (recall that male *costae* have large breeding territories). Assuming that the male in whose territory the female nests has in fact mated with that female, this situation provides an exceptionally clear demonstration of the selective value of control of a food supply by a territorial male. This argument has been developed in greater detail by Wolf and Stiles (1970) for an even more striking example of this phenomenon in *Panterpe insignis*. In effect, this situation is taking the process of aggressive selection, as proposed above for *anna*, one step further. In neither of these cases is there ever any suggestion of the male hummingbird helping the female in the actual chores of nesting. In fact, in the case of *costae*, the male is a decided hindrance to the female. A *costae* male will chase and display at any female who appears conspicuously in his territory. Female *costae* in this situation often have to make wide, low-flying detours to reach the nest as inconspicuously as possible.

When floral food resources are scarce or localized and/or energy needs are high, intraspecific competition at flowers may be severe. Male hummingbirds are usually dominant to females, and with such an individualistic social system the females may suffer in competition for food. Hummingbirds have evolved two strategies for relieving the ecological pressure on females at these times:

spatial separation of the sexes and changes in relative dominance of the sexes (Stiles and Wolf, 1970). The first is exemplified by different habitat preferences of males and females of many North American hummingbirds during the breeding season: *Calypte anna* is an excellent example. Such species are often sexually dimorphic, much of the selection for reproductive fitness being intrasexual (e.g., aggressive selction).

Equal dominance of the sexes is seen in many tropical hummingbirds during the nonbreeding season, when females hold feeding territories on an essentially equal footing with males (Wolf, 1969; Stiles and Wolf, 1970). Because there presumably has been selection for similarity in modes of territorial defense at these times, many such species show little or no sexual dichromatism. An example is *Panterpe insignis*, in which the effects of aggressive selection during the breeding season are apparently offset by selection for equal dominance at other times. However, males in breeding condition may have songs or displays not seen in other seasons, perhaps reflecting differences in dominance between the sexes during reproduction. *Panterpe* probably fits in here, and the various *Amazilia* species almost certainly do (see Skutch in Bent, 1940 for a typical example).

A complementary example may be provided by the Rufous Hummingbird during migration. As discussed above, in the Santa Monica Mountains there is no noticeable difference in timing or dominance of the sexes. Males, however, usually arrive on the breeding grounds first (Bent, 1940), and are presumably dominant there. In my study areas display activity of male *rufus* is greater among later migrants than earlier ones. Displays by male *rufus* are also apparently more common at Berkeley, 400 miles closer to the breeding grounds (Ortiz, 1967). Taken together, these observations suggest a progressive increase in dominance of male *rufus* as they approach the breeding grounds, which is reflected in the different arrival times of the sexes. That *rufus* is sexually dichromatic would, on this view, be due to aggressive selection on the breeding grounds overriding the effects of selection for equal dominance of the sexes in migration.

Starting with the typical monogamous pair-bond of most birds, aggressive selection can operate to produce a mating system strikingly similar to that of *Panterpe*: females mating with males holding the best territories and nesting therein, and the males with the best territories getting the most females. The most important requisite for such a system seems to be a very localized or patchy distribution of resources (food, nest sites, etc.), such that different males may control territories of widely varying amounts of these resources (Verner and Willson, 1966). Orians (1969) notes that if such be the case, and if the female can usually rear a normal clutch of young without help from the male, then polygamy or promiscuity is a self-accelerating system, with selection acting on the male for the ability to control better territories. Such polygamy will be advantageous for the female also, if the advantage of mating with a male on a good territory, even though he may already have a mate, exceeds the disadvantage of not having his help in raising the young (Verner, 1964). Most North American passerines with polygamous mating systems appear to fit these conditions (Verner and Willson, 1966; Orians, 1969; see also Crook, 1965).

On this basis, one might have expected that polygamous or promiscuous mating systems would be widespread among nectar-feeding birds. In fact, except for the hummingbirds, every nectarivorous bird yet studied appears to be monogamous. This includes a scattering of honeycreepers (Skutch, 1954; Biaggi, 1955; de Carvalho, 1958), sunbirds (Van Someren, 1956; Broekhuysen, 1963; Skead, 1967), honeyeaters and sugarbirds (Gwynne, 1948; Broekhuysen, 1959; Skead, 1963). Dispersion of food supply and competition have yet to be considered as potential factors in the evolution of social behavior of Old World or South American nectarivores, and basic ecological and behavioral information is available for only a very few species. Therefore, the striking differences in social organization between hummingbirds and other nectarivorous birds cannot be satisfactorily explained on the basis of current information. However, the available data do suggest several possible approaches to the problem.

The first and most obvious point is that hummingbirds are morphologically and behaviorally much more specialized for nectar feeding than any other bird group. Among the relevant specializations are small size, manner of flight, bill and tongue morphology, and inability to walk, hop, or hold objects in the feet. Hummingbirds are specialized to the point where many kinds of potential foods—fruit, seeds, any but the smallest insects—are practically unavailable to them. Most honeycreepers, sunbirds, and honeyeaters take varying amounts of fruit and a much wider spectrum of insects than do hummingbirds. Conversely, many of these other nectar-feeders seem much less dependent on flowers during the breeding season than do hummingbirds. Certain honeycreepers (Skutch, 1954; Biaggi, 1955), sunbirds (Broekhuysen, 1953; Skead, 1967), and honeyeaters (Gwynne, 1948) are relatively more insectivorous and/or frugivorous during the breeding season, but visit flowers freely at other times (see also Keast, 1968; Lack, 1968). However, nectar is still an important food of breeding adults and young of at least some sunbirds (Van Someren, 1956; Skead, 1967), honeyeaters (Broekhuysen, 1959), and honeycreepers (Skutch, 1954; Biaggi, 1955).

Many of the discussions of the habits of sunbirds and honeyeaters give one the impression that the flowers upon which they feed often occur in more continuous expanses or in larger, richer patches than do most hummingbird food plants. There are repeated references to broad fields or mountainsides full of such flowers as *Aloe*, *Protea*, etc., in Africa (e.g., Broekhuysen, 1959 and 1963; Skead, 1963 and 1967; Chapin, 1954) and to large stands of *Eucalyptus*, *Banksia*, etc., in Australia (Gannon, 1962; Keast, 1968, among others). Also, relatively more of the ornithophilous plants of Africa and Australia appear to be trees—often of considerable size (*Eucalyptus*, *Symphonia*, *Erythrina*, etc.). In my experience, large ornithophilous trees are exceptional in tropical Middle America and absent in North America: most bird-pollinated plants of these areas are herbs, shrubs, or epiphytes (see also Grant and Grant, 1968; Ruschi, 1949). Also, such flowers seldom cover anything larger than a small meadow continuously. It may be that many Old World flowers represent less of a localized food source; or they may come in bigger patches that can often support more individuals. Under these circumstances, advantages of a highly individualistic social system like that of hummingbirds may be much reduced. This may also be the reason why most of the seasonal movements of nectarivores other than hummingbirds are made by family groups or small flocks rather than individuals, and why feeding territoriality is so seldom seen in these groups.

One of the prerequisites mentioned by Orians (1969) for the evolution of polygamy is that clutch-size be limited by factors other than the ability of the parent(s) to rear young. All hummingbirds have a clutch of 2, and this appears to be determined by factors associated with nest size, as will be discussed elsewhere; in no hummingbird does the male consistently provide direct help in nesting (cf. Ruschi, 1965). In other nectar feeders, the role of the male varies from essentially nil to almost equal to that of the female. The sunbirds discussed by Van Someren (1956) provide a very interesting case in point. In species of the genera *Anthreptes* and *Cinnyris*, the role of the male is considerable, and the clutch size is 2. In *Nectarinia famosa* and *kilimensis*, the female carries out the nesting duties alone, and the clutch size is 1. Males of the *Nectarinia* species are much more aggressive than the others, holding feeding territories in the non-breeding season; *Cinnyris* are paired year-round, and *Anthreptes* are still more social. *Nectarinia* spp. are the most nectarivorous, *Anthreptes* spp. the least. *Chalcostigma* spp. appear more or less intermediate in all respects, and the clutch size varies from 1 to 2. In view of the above correlations, polygamy may well be expected in *Nectarinia* and perhaps *Chalcostigma*; and the relative dispersions of food resources merit detailed consideration. Further ecological and behavioral studies on these birds could be exceedingly rewarding.

Nectar-feeding Birds and Man

As discussed above, man has had considerable effects upon the breeding and seasonal movements of California hummingbirds in space, but not in time. This appears to be true of other nectar-feeding birds as well. All over the world, these birds have been quick to take advantage of changes in the spatial distribution of floral food resources caused by man. By the introduction of potential food flowers, man can greatly increase the density of breeding nectarivores, or can make available areas previously unsuitable for breeding (Skead, 1967; Ruschi, 1949). In seasons where native flowers are scarce, nectar-feeding birds are quick to utilize introduced ones, and this may affect the extent and duration of seasonal movements (Skead, 1967; Hobbs, 1961), or the proportion of the population undertaking such movements (Wagner, 1945). Although no quantitative data are available, it seems likely that man has increased the populations of many species of nectar-feeding birds by providing flowers that bloom during periods of scarcity of native food plants. Many nectarivorous birds are known to resort to gardens or introduced plants like *Nicotiana* at such times (Skead, 1963 and 1967; Hobbs, 1961; Serventy and Whittell, 1951; and many others). In no area, however, has there been any suggestion of a major shift in the timing of breeding or seasonal movements occasioned by man's introduction of potential food plants.

Ornithophilous plants are especially likely to be introduced by man because of their usually showy flowers, as witness the popularity of such plants as *Strelitzia*, *Aloe*, *Fuchsia*, *Callistemon*, *Abutilon*, and *Erythrina* in California. Ornithophilous plants transported to different parts of the world are quickly found and utilized by the local nectar-feeding birds, even when there are decided disparities in bill and corolla morphology (Skead, 1967; van der Pijl, 1937). For example, *Nicotiana glauca* has been introduced into South Africa and Australia, where its nectar is extensively utilized by sunbirds and honeyeaters, respectively (Skead, 1967; Hobbs, 1961). In North America, *Nicotiana* is now found south to central Mexico, and I have seen it visited by *Amazilia rutila* and *A. violiceps* in Sonora and Sinaloa. The various species of *Eucalyptus* are staple foods of various Australian honeyeaters (Serventy and Whittell, 1951; Gannon, 1962; Keast, 1968). Introduced into North and South America, *Eucalyptus* is freely visited by hummingbirds and other nectar-feeders such as orioles and coerebids (Ruschi, 1949; present report). In South Africa *Eucalyptus* is avidly visited by sunbirds (Skead, 1967). *Eucalyptus* and *Nicotiana* have apparently escaped from cultivation and become naturalized in many parts of the world, and it would be exceedingly interesting to compare their roles in the ecology and annual cycles of nectar-feeding birds in different areas. In particular, it would be interesting to see whether these plants have benefited the populations of other nectarivorous birds to the extent that they have the Anna Hummingbird.

SUMMARY AND CONCLUSIONS

This paper reports the results of a three-year study of the ecology of the Anna Hummingbird (*Calypte anna*) in the Santa Monica Mountains, Los Angeles County, California. The overall objective was to assess the role of food supply in determining the occurrence, in space and time, of territorial behavior, breeding, and seasonal movements. The major conclusions are as follows:

1. The initiation of breeding in male Anna Hummingbirds can be divided into several components. Testicular maturation and the first appearance of breeding behavior are very closely correlated with the onset of the winter rains. The actual movement into the chaparral to take up breeding territories is dependent upon the appearance of a suitable food supply, *Ribes malvaceum*, which also begins to bloom immediately after the first winter rains. Full breeding behavior (persistent song from exposed perches, consistent defense of the entire breeding territory by long chases and display dives) is attained independently of the first appearance of breeding territoriality or acquisition of a territory. The timing of the first heavy winter rains varied widely from year to year during this study, but full breeding behavior appeared in *anna* males at about the same time each year. This suggests the existence of a photoperiod-sensitive system that regulates the time span during which *anna* males can attain full breeding condition following rainfall.

2. Some male *anna* can obtain all of their food on territory, while others must commute to other feeding areas for part or all of their food. Competition for territories that contain a food supply is more intense than for those that do not. Territories containing ample food may be more advantageous as mating stations, as it is thought that food may attract females to the males' territories, and females may prefer to mate with males controlling the best territories.

3. Because nesting female *anna* apparently do not utilize nocturnal torpor as an energy-saving device, they are dependent upon a convenient nectar source during the early phases of nesting. The distribution of suitable flowers often influences the female's choice of nest site. The defense of these flowers during the early part of the nesting cycle is the closest approach shown by female *anna* to the feeding territoriality of male *anna*. When flowers are highly localized and controlled by territorial males, a female hummingbird may nest in or near the territory of a male, although his part in the nesting effort itself is one of interference, rather than aid.

4. Juvenile *anna* show territorial behavior at a very early age, as well as what appears to be play behavior fully comparable to that described in young mammals.

Precocious territorial behavior is probably adaptive in that it enables the young juveniles to obtain control over good feeding areas, thus rendering the critical postfledging period less hazardous than it might otherwise be. Sometimes juvenile *anna* or migratory *Selasphorus* obtain control of a feeding area controlled by an adult male *anna*, by "swamping" out the male by sheer numbers and persistence. Territorial male *anna* are always dominant to juvenile *anna* or migratory *S. rufus* on an individual basis, however.

5. Breeding territoriality in *anna* males breaks down during April and May, at a time when food sources in general are increasing, but the flower with the most abundant nectar is rapidly declining. This factor, combined with the augmented energy demands of defending a territory against increasing numbers of *anna* juveniles and hummingbirds of other species, appears to erode the effectiveness of a territorial male. The annual molt, commencing in April, may not play a direct role in decline of breeding territory, but it is a definite indicator of the general physiological condition of the bird at this time. There is marked geographic variation in the timing of molt and breeding in *C. anna*.

6. The timing of the appearance of large numbers of juveniles on the territories of adult male *anna* is in large part a reflection of reproductive success earlier in the breeding season. Since these young birds play an important part in the breakdown of breeding territoriality in adult males, their appearance in numbers functions as a negative feedback, tending to inhibit further reproduction. There is some evidence that the progeny of very late broods have a greatly reduced chance of reproductive success during the following breeding season.

7. The reproductive seasons of *Calypte anna* and *Ribes speciosum* depart in a similar manner from those of most chaparral birds and plants, respectively. During the cold winter months, *anna* depends on *speciosum* for food, *speciosum* on *anna* for pollination: winter reproduction in either species would be impossible without the other. It is likely that the reproductive seasons of *anna* and *speciosum* evolved together, along with certain morphological coadaptations. Hummingbird pollination may be more advantageous than insect pollination in cold climates generally (including tropical highland areas, where the greatest taxonomic and ecological diversity of hummingbirds occurs). A number of other hummingbirds breed at the coldest and/or wettest times of year in various tropical regions, and for most of these there appears to be a close ecological relationship between breeding and the blooming of certain food plants, comparable to the relationship between *C. anna* and *R. speciosum*. In most hummingbirds and many other nectar-feeders, the most important ultimate factor regulating breeding seasonality is the need to have the young fledge when flowers (as opposed to insects) are most abundant. In *C. anna* the early nesting season may be important in allowing the first broods to fledge, become independent, and occupy feeding territories before the arrival of large numbers of spring migrant hummingbirds.

8. The distribution of flowers in time and space is the crucial factor regulatiug the timing, direction, and extent of seasonal movements of nectar-feeding birds. Nectarivores tend to wander more widely than other trophic groups of small land birds because of the highly localized, stationary, conspicuous, and temporally restricted nature of their food source.

9. Through his introduction of such fall-blooming flowers as *Nicotiana* and *Eucalyptus* man has increased the carrying capacity of chaparral regions during a critical period of the year, probably resulting in a great increase in population size in the Anna Hummingbird. Increasing the food supply by the addition of introduced flowers can, on the local level, greatly increase the number of breeding hummingbirds, but seems to have had relatively minor effects on timing of breeding and seasonal movements, and nesting success. The hazards of migration may be reduced because of the increase in food available along the way. Migration routes themselves are little affected except on the local level, but the proportion of the population undertaking migration may be markedly altered. Man has affected the ecology and annual cycles of other nectar-feeding birds in an apparently similar way in other areas. Certain ornithophilous plants such as *Nicotiana* and *Eucalyptus* have been introduced in many parts of the world, and have often become naturalized; the effects of these plants on the ecology of other nectar-feeders should be studied.

10. Hummingbirds are unusual among nectar-feeding birds in their highly individualistic social organization, including their promiscuous mating system. Other nectarivores studied so far, in various passerine families, are monogamous; they tend to flock in the nonbreeding season, and rarely hold feeding territories. Further study is required to explain these differences. Among the factors that should be considered are differences in the degree of morphological and behavioral specialization for nectar-feeding, relative dependence on nectar vs. insects during the breeding season, capacity of the female to rear the young unaided by the male, and differences in the dispersion of floral food resources.

LITERATURE CITED

BALDWIN, S. P., H. C. OBERHOLSER, and L. G. WORLEY.
1931. Measurements of birds. Sci. Publ. Cleveland Mus. Nat. Hist., Vol. II. 165 pp.

BAUER, H. L.
1936. Moisture relations in the chaparral of the Santa Monica Mountains, California. Ecol. Monogr. 6:409-453.

BENE, F.
1946. Feeding and related behaviors of hummingbirds. Mem. Boston Nat. His. Soc. 9:403-481.

BENT, A. C.
1940. Life Histories of North American cuckoos, goatsuckers, hummingbirds, and their allies. Bull. U.S. Nat'l. Mus. 176:319-491.

BIAGGI, V.
1955. The Puerto Rican Honeycreeper (Reinita), *Coereba flaveola portoricensis* (Bryant). Publ. of Univ. of Puerto Rico Agr. Exp't'l. Station, Rio Piedras, Puerto Rico. 61 pp.

BOWLES, J. H.
1910. The Anna Hummingbird. Condor 12:125-127.

BROEKHUYSEN, G. J.
1959. The biology of the Cape Sugarbird, *Promerops cafer* (L.) Proc. 1st Pan-Afr. Ornithol: Congr., Ostrich Suppl. 3:180-221.
1963. The breeding biology of the Orange-breasted Sunbird, *Anthobaphes violacea*. Ostrich 34:187-234.

BROWN, J. L.
1964. The evolution of diversity in avian territorial systems. Wilson Bull. 76:160-169.

BUTTERWORTH, H. M.
1964. Dates of introduction of trees and shrubs into California. Dept. of Landscape Horticulture, Univ. of California, Davis. 11 pp.

CHAPIN, J. P.
1932. Birds of the Belgian Congo, Vol. I. Bull. Amer. Mus. Nat. Hist. 65. 756 pp.
1954. Birds of the Belgian Congo, Vol. IV. Bull. Amer. Mus. Nat. Hist. 75*B*. 832 pp.
1959. Breeding cycles of *Nectarinia purpureiventris* and some other Kivu birds. Proc. 1st Pan-Afr. Ornithol. Congr., Ostrich Suppl. 3:222-229.

CHAPMAN, F. M.
1926. The distribution of bird-life in Ecuador. Bull. Amer. Mus. Nat. Hist. 55. 784 pp.

CHILDS, H. E., JR.
1968. The Brown Towhees. Pp. 603-620 *in* A. C. Bent, et al., Life Histories of North American cardinals, grosbeaks, buntings, towhees, finches, sparrows, and allies. Compiled and edited by O. L. Austin, Jr. U.S. Nat'l. Mus., Bull. 237.

CODY, M. L.
1968. Interspecific territoriality among hummingbird species. Condor 70:270-271.

COLE, N. H. A.
1967. Comparative physiological ecology of the genus *Eriogonum* in the Santa Monica Mountains, southern California. Ecol. Monogr. 37:1-24.

COOPER, W. S.
1922. The broad sclerophyll vegetation of California. Car. Inst. Wash. Publ. 319:1-124.

CROOK, J. H.
  1965. The adaptive significance of avian social organizations. Symp. Zool. Soc. Lond. 14: 182-218.
DAWSON, W. L.
  1923. The Birds of California. Los Angeles: South Moulton Co., Vol. II:915-960, 1112-1119.
DE CARVALHO, C. T.
  1958. Notas ecologicas sobre *Coereba flaveola* (Passeres, Coerebidae). Bol. Mus. Paraense Emilio Goeldi 10:1-21.
ERICKSON, M. M.
  1938. Territory, annual cycle, and numbers in a population of Wren-tits (*Chamaea fasciata*). Univ. of Calif. Publ., Zool. 42:247-334.
GANNON, G. R.
  1962. Distribution of the Australian Honeyeaters. Emu 62:145-166.
GRANT, K. A., and V. GRANT.
  1967. Effects of hummingbird migration on plant speciation in the California flora. Evolution 21:457-465.
  1968. Hummingbirds and their flowers. New York: Columbia University Press.
GRINNELL, J.
  1908. Biota of the San Bernardino Mountains. Univ. of Calif. Publ., Zool. 5:1-170.
GRINNELL, J. and A. H. MILLER.
  1944. The distribution of the birds of California. Pacific Coast Avifauna 27:216-225.
GRINNELL, J., and H. S. SWARTH.
  1913. Birds and mammals of the San Jacinto area of southern California. Univ. Calif. Publ., Zool. 10:197-406.
GWYNNE, A. J.
  1948. Notes on the Brown Honeyeater. Emu 47:161-164.
HANES, T. L.
  1965. Ecological studies on two closely related shrubs in southern California. Ecol. Monogr. 35:213-236.
HANES, T. L., and H. W. JONES.
  1967. Postfire chaparral succession in southern California. Ecology 48:259-265.
HOBBS, J. N.
  1958. Association between the Black Honeyeater and the Emu Bush. Emu 58:127-129.
  1961. The birds of southwest New South Wales. Emu 61:21-55.
  1967. Honeyeaters and Emu Bush, *Eremophila*. Emu 66:386-388.
HOWELL, T. R., and W. R. DAWSON.
  1954. Nest temperatures and attentiveness in the Anna Hummingbird. Condor 56:93-97.
HUXLEY, J. S.
  1938. Darwin's theory of sexual selection and the data subsumed by it, in the light of recent research. Amer. Nat. 72:416-433.
JEPSON, W. L.
  1925. A manual of the flowering plants of California. 3d printing, 1957. Berkeley: Univ. of Calif. Press. 1238 pp.
KEAST, A.
  1968. Seasonal movements in the Australian Honeyeaters (Meliphagidae) and their ecological significance. Emu 67:159-209.
LACK, D. L.
  1954. The natural regulation of animal numbers. Oxford: Clarendon Press.
  1966. Population studies of birds. Oxford: Clarendon Press.
  1968. Ecological adaptations for breeding in birds. London: Methuen.

Lasiewski, R. L.
 1963. Oxygen consumption of torpid, resting, active, and flying hummingbirds. Physical. Zool. 36:124-140.
Legg, K., and F. A. Pitelka.
 1956. Ecologic overlap of Allen and Anna Hummingbirds nesting at Santa Cruz, California. Condor 58:393-405.
Lehrman, D. S.
 1964. Control of behavior cycles in reproduction. Pp. 143-156 *in* Etkin, W., ed., Social behavior and organization among vertebrates. Chicago: Univ. of Chicago Press.
Lofts, B., and R. K. Murton.
 1968. Photoperiodic and physiological adaptations regulating avian breeding cycles, and their ecological significance. J. Zool. 155:327-394.
Loizos, C.
 1966. Play in mammals. Pp. 1-9 *in* P. A. Jewell and C. Loizos, eds., Play, exploration, and territory in mammals. Symp. Zool. Soc. London 18:1-9.
MacMillen, R. E.
 1964. Population ecology, water relations, and social behavior of a Southern California semi-desert rodent fauna. Univ. of Calif. Publ., Zool. 71:1-61.
Marler, P. and W. J. Hamilton III.
 1966. Mechanisms of animal behavior. New York: John Wiley and Sons.
Marshall, A. J.
 1961. Breeding seasons and migration. Pp. 307-340 *in* A. J. Marshall, ed., Biology and comparative physiology of birds. New York: Academic Press.
Marshall, A. J. and H. S. Disney.
 1957. Experimental induction of breeding in a xerophilous bird. Nature 180:647.
Mason, W. A.
 1965. The social development of monkeys and apes. In I. DeVore, ed., Primate behavior. New York: Holt, Rinehart and Winston.
McMinn, H. E.
 1959. An illustrated manual of California shrubs. Berkeley: Univ. of Calif. Press.
Miller, E. H.
 1947. Growth and environmental conditions in the southern California chaparral. Amer-Midland Nat. 37:379-420.
Miller, E. V.
 1941. Behavior of the Bewick Wren. Condor 43:81-99.
Moynihan, M.
 1963. Inter-specific relations between some Andean birds. Ibis 105:327-339.
Orians, G. H.
 1961. The ecology of Blackbird (*Agelaius*) social systems. Ecol. Monogr. 31:285-312.
 1969. On the evolution of mating systems in birds and mammals. Amer. Nat. 103:589-604.
Orians, G. H., and G. E. Collier.
 1963. Competition and Blackbird social systems. Evolution 17:449-459.
Ortiz-Crespo, F. I.
 1967. Interactions in three sympatric species of California hummingbirds in a planted area containing melliferous flowering vegetation. Unpublished M. A. thesis, University of California, Berkeley. 161 pp.
Padilla, V.
 1961. Southern California gardens: an illustrated history. Berkeley: Univ. of Calif. Press.
Pearson, O. P.
 1950. The metabolism of hummingbirds. Condor 52:145-152.
 1954. The daily energy requirements of a wild Anna Hummingbird. Condor 56:317-322.

PERCIVAL, M.
    1961. Types of nectar in Angiosperms. New Phytologist 60:235-281.

PILLSBURY, A. F., J. F. OSBORN, and R. E. PELESHEK.
    1963. Residual soil moisture below root zone in Southern California watersheds. J. Geophys. Res. 68, no. 4.

PIMENTEL, R. A.
    1960 Inter- and intrahabitat movements of the Rough-skinned Newt, *Taricha torosa granulosa* (Skilton). Amer. Midland Nat. 63:470-496.

PITELKA, F. A.
    1942. Territoriality and related problems in North American hummingbirds. Condor 44:189-203.
    1951a. Ecologic overlap and interspecific strife in breeding populations of Anna and Allen Hummingbirds. Ecology 32:641-661.
    1951b. Breeding seasons of hummingbirds at Santa Barbara, California. Condor 53:198-201.

RAVEN, P. H., and H. J. THOMPSON.
    1966. Flora of the Santa Monica Mountains, California. University of California, Los Angeles: unpublished manuscript. 185 pp.

RIPLEY, S. D.
    1959. Competition between sunbird and honeyeater species in the Moluccan Islands. Amer. Nat. 93:127-132.

RUSCHI, A.
    1949. A polinização realizada pelos Trochilideos, a sua área de alimentação e o repovoamento. Bol. Mus. Biol. Prof. Mello-Leitão 2:1-51.
    1950. O território e as áreas de alimentação e de nidificação de *Anisoterus pretrei* (Delattre and Lesson), observadas atraves algumas gerações. Bol. Mus. Biol. Prof. Mello-Leitão 8:1-20.
    1967. Beija-flores das matas, dos scrubs, das savanas, dos campos e grasslands do Brasil e a sua Zoogeografia. Bol. Mus. Biol. Prof. Mello-Leitao 51:1-23.

SARGENT, G. T.
    1940. Observations on the behavior of color-banded California Thrashers. Condor 42:49-60.

SAUNDERS, A. A.
    1936. Ecology of the birds of Quaker Run Valley, Allegany State Park, New York. N.Y. State Mus. Hbk. 16:1-174.

SELANDER, R. K.
    1965. On mating systems and sexual selection. Am. Nat. 99:129-141.

SERVENTY, D. L., and H. M. WHITTELL.
    1951. Birds of Western Australia, 2d ed. Perth, Australia: Paterson Press.

SKEAD, C. J.
    1967. The Sunbirds of Southern Africa. Capetown, S. Africa: Cape and Transvaal Printers.

SKEAD, D. M.
    1963. Gurney's Sugarbird, *Promerops gurneyi* Verreaux, *in* The Natal Drakensberg. Ostrich 34:160-164.

SKINNER, M. P.
    1938. The Pacific Great Horned Owl. Pp. 333-341 *in* A. C. Bent, Life Histories of North American Birds of Prey, Part I. U.S. Nat'l. Mus., Bull. 170.

SKUTCH, A. F.
    1950 The nesting seasons of Central American birds in relation to climate and food supply. Ibis 92:185-222.
    1954. Life Histories of Central American Birds, Vol. I. Pac. Coast Avif., no. 31. 448 pp.
    1966. A breeding bird census and nesting success in Central America. Ibis 108:1-16.
    1967. Life histories of Central American highland birds. Publ. Nuttall Orn. Club, no. 7.

Smith, G. T. C.
   1969. A high altitude hummingbird on the Volcano Cotopaxi. Ibis 111:17-22.
Snell, M. L.
   1963. Birds at 7000 feet in an area of montane grassland on the eastern border of Southern Rhodesia. Ostrich 34:36-39.
Snow, D. W., and B. K. Snow.
   1964. Breeding seasons and annual cycles of Trinidad land-birds. Zoologica 49:1-39.
Stebbins, R. C.
   1951. Amphibians of western North America. Berkeley: Univ. of Calif. Press. 539 pp.
Stiles, F. G.
   1971a. Time, energy, and territoriality of the Anna Hummingbird. Science 173:818-821.
   1971b. On the field identification of California hummingbirds. Calif. Birds 2:41-54.
   1972. Age and sex determination in Rufous and Allen Hummingbirds. Condor 74:25-32.
Stiles, F. G., and L. L. Wolf.
   1970. Hummingbird territoriality at a tropical flowering tree. Auk 87:467-491.
Thomson, A. L.
   1950. Factors determining the breeding seasons of birds: an introductory review. Ibis 92: 173-184.
van der Pijl, L.
   1937. Disharmony between Asiatic flower-birds and American bird-flowers. Ann. Jard. Bot. Buitenzorg 48:17-26.
van Rossem, A. J.
   1945. Eastern distributional limits of the Anna Hummingbird in winter. Condor 47:79-80.
Van Someren, V. G. L.
   1956. Days with birds: studies of the habits of some East African species. Fieldiana: Zool. 38:434-451.
Verner, J.
   1964. Evolution of polygamy in the Long-billed Marsh Wren. Evolution 28:252-261.
Verner, J., and M. F. Willson.
   1966. The influence of habitats on mating systems of North American passerine birds. Ecology 47:143-147.
Vuilleumier, F.
   1969. Systematics and evolution in *Diglossa* (Aves, Coerebidae). Amer. Mus. Novitates 2381. 44 pp.
Wagner, H. O.
   1945. Notes on the life history of the Mexican Violet-ear. Wilson Bull. 57:165-187.
Willett, G.
   1912. Birds of the Pacific slope of Southern California. Pacific Coast Avifauna, no. 7:59-62.
Williamson, F. S. L.
   1956. The molt and testis cycle of the Anna Hummingbird. Condor 58:342-366.
Wolf, L. L.
   1969. Female territoriality in a tropical hummingbird. Auk 86:490-504.
   1970. The impact of seasonal flowering on the biology of some tropical hummingbirds. Condor 72:1-14.
Wolf, L. L., and F. G. Stiles.
   1970. The evolution of pair cooperation in a tropical hummingbird. Evolution 24:776-790.
Woods, R. S.
   1927. The hummingbirds of California. Auk 44:297-318.
   1940. The Anna Hummingbird. Pp. 371-387 *in* A. C., Bent, Life histories of North American cuckoos, goatsuckers, hummingbirds and their allies. U.S. Nat'l. Mus., Bull. 176.
   1948. The California Thrasher. Pp. 402-410 *in* A. C., Bent, Life histories of North American nuthatches, wrens, thrashers and their allies. U.S. Nat'l. Mus., Bull. 195.

PLATES

PLATE 1

Flowers of the two *Ribes* species important in the annual cycle of the Anna Hummingbird.

A. *Ribes malvaceum*. The flowers are pink, the corolla tube ca. 5 mm. in length.

B. *Ribes speciosum*. The flowers are bright red, becoming crimson with age. Length of corolla tube ca. 12 mm. Note the small, shiny leaves and thorny twigs.

PLATE 2

Franklin Canyon study area.

A. Aerial photograph of Franklin Canyon Reservoir and surrounding areas. The ridgetop site is to the left. Note the planted areas at both ends of the reservoir, and the orange grove at lower right.

B. Chaparral habitat along the ridgetop study site: this slope contained the core areas of breeding territories of *anna* males A(1967-68), 1(1968-69) and III(1969-70); cf. figure 10. This area is at the extreme upper left of the above aerial photograph.

PLATE 3

Stone Canyon study area.

A. Aerial photograph of the grounds of Stone Canyon Reservoir. The garden grove is just above center; the *Eucalyptus* grove just below center. Chaparral slopes upon which male *anna* held breeding territories are at top.

B. The interior of the garden grove. Most of the trees visible are alders; *Heliconia* on both sides of the path at center.

PLATE 4

Trancas Canyon study area.

A. Aerial photograph of Trancas Canyon. The oak-sycamore woodland at center. Oaks are distinguished by their thick foliage and rounded crowns; sycamores by their tall, straight, light-colored trunks (during the winter, sycamores lose their leaves but oaks do not).

B. Oak (*Quercus agrifolia*) woodland in Trancas Canyon. The small shrubs around the base of the trees at center are *Ribes speciosum*.

WITHDRAWN